SERIES EDITOR: LEE JOH

ELITE 70

ELIZABETHAN SEA DOGS 1560-1605

TEXT BY
ANGUS KONSTAM

COLOUR PLATES BY
ANGUS McBRIDE

OSPREY
MILITARY

First published in Great Britain in 2000 by Osprey Publishing , Elms Court, Chapel Way, Botley, Oxford OX2 9LP United Kingdom
Email: info@ospreypublishing.com

ISBN 1 84176 015 3

Editor: Anita Hitchings
Design: Alan Hamp
Originated by Grasmere Digital Imaging Ltd, Leeds, UK
Printed in China through World Print Ltd

00 01 02 03 04   10 9 8 7 6 5 4 3 2 1

For a Catalogue of all books published by Osprey Military, Automotive and Aviation please write to:
The Marketing Manager, Osprey Publishing Ltd., P.O. Box 140, Wellingborough, Northants NN8 4ZA United Kingdom
Email: **info@ospreydirect.co.uk**

The Marketing Manager, Osprey Direct USA, P.O. Box 130, Sterling Heights, MI 48311-0130, United States of America
Email: **info@ospreydirectusa.com**

Or visit Osprey at:
www.ospreypublishing.com

Acknowledgements

Then following institutions, individuals and organisations were particularly useful in providing source material for this work, or allowing access to their collections or archives: Archivas de la Contraction, Seville, Spain; Archivo General de Simancas, Spain; the Alderney Wreck Project (Michael Bowyer); British Library, London (Department of Manuscripts); Mariners Museum, Newport News, Virginia; *Mary Rose* Trust, Portsmouth; Mel Fisher Maritime Museum, Key West, Florida; National Museum of Ireland, Dublin; National Maritime Museum, Greenwich, London; Public Record Office, Kew, London; Royal Armouries, Leeds; Royal Arsenal Museum, Woolwich, London; Scottish Institute for Maritime Studies, St Andrews University (Dr Colin Martin); Ulster Museums, Belfast.

Note: The following abbreviations are used in the picture captions throughout the book;
Mariners – Mariners' Museum, Newport News, Virginia
MAS - Museum of Arts and Sciences, Daytona Beach, Florida
MFMHS – Mel Fisher Maritime Heritage Society, Key West, Florida
NMM – National Maritime Museum, Greenwich, England
NYPL – New York Public Library, Rare Book Division
PRO - Public Record Office, London, England

Artist's Note

TITLE PAGE **Sir Francis Drake (c.1540-96) wearing full armour, from a contemporary German engraving. Although half-armour was sometimes worn in action, it was the exception rather than the rule. (John Carter Brown Library, Brown University, Providence, Rhode Island)**

ELIZABETHAN SEA DOGS 1560-1605

INTRODUCTION

THE PHRASE 'SEA DOGS' summons up images of swashbucklers, plunder on the high seas and England's sailors standing up against the overwhelming might of Spain. The era when mariners sailed as privateers, explorers, merchants or in the service of Queen Elizabeth is one of the most colourful in English history, and has been the subject of numerous books and films. Although the basic history of the defeat of the Spanish Armada and the raids of Sir Francis Drake on the Spanish Main is well known, a combination of nationalism and a lack of knowledge about the available source material has resulted in a very stilted view of the period. The 'Sea Dogs'; adventurers such as Drake, Hawkins, Raleigh and Frobisher, were not always as successful as the writers of Victorian histories would have us believe, and their actions were often influenced by profit rather than by any feeling of patriotic duty. The emphasis on English naval heroes has almost obscured the fact that the Dutch and the French were also actively engaged in the often undeclared war against the Spanish empire, and many of the greatest successes of the Elizabethan heroes were brought about through co-operation with these Protestant allies. The much-maligned Spanish could also boast of a number of successes against their adversaries, and the actions of commanders such as Juan Martinez de Recalde and Pedro Menendez de Aviles have almost gone unnoticed outside Spain.

In recent years, improved access to Spanish historical material such as the archives in Simancas and Seville has helped to redress the balance, providing a chance to examine the era through Spanish eyes. Similarly, recent developments in underwater archaeology have provided scholars with a rare opportunity to discover what life was like on board the warships of the Elizabethan era, or the Spanish vessels which sailed as part of the Armada or carried the treasures of the New World back to Spain. Although the scope of this work means that the author can do little more than

Sir Walter Raleigh (c.1552-1618) with Spanish prisoners following his attack on the port of St Josef in Trinidad in 1594. Although he was leading a voyage of exploration at the time, Raleigh seized the opportunity to attack the Spanish when the opportunity presented itself. Engraving by Theodore de Bry. (NYPL)

cover the basic outline of the subject, this brief overview is the result of extensive primary archival research over a period of 15 years, and incorporates information from scores of sources in museums, archives and archaeological collections. Much of this information runs contrary to the established view of the Elizabethan 'sea dogs' and their modus operandi. By ignoring myth and focusing on substantiated original material, it is hoped that an objective view of the world of Drake and Hawkins can be achieved, shorn of the baggage imposed by jingoism and Hollywood.

THE ELIZABETHAN 'SEA DOGS'

To the Spanish, men like Drake and Hawkins were pirates, and if caught would be treated as such. To the English, the legal status of these 'sea dogs' was often vague and, technically at least, many of their actions strayed from privateering into the realms of piracy. The circumstances which permitted them to get away with piracy were unique, and to the eyes of much of English society, their actions were considered perfectly acceptable. Many late-16th-century English seamen regarded trade and plunder as inseparable, performed by all kinds of men, from smugglers and cut-throats to the nobility, taking forms which varied from legitimate privateering to unrestricted piracy. During this period, Elizabethan sea-plunder became increasingly identified with patriotic motives, and with the struggle to maintain the Protestant religion.

The difference between a pirate and a privateer is that a privateer attacks the enemies of his country under license from the government, while a pirate attacks anybody, irrespective of nationality. In theory, attacks on Spanish ships by men who did not hold a privateering licence were acts of piracy, but as the authorities usually turned a blind eye or even condoned these attacks, the state was effectively giving its illicit support to piracy. In western England piracy was partly legitimised by support from the gentry and local authorities. Piracy still existed, but increasingly the Crown ceased to condemn the pirates, provided they attacked foreign ships, preferably Spanish ones. Small-scale piracy continued to thrive throughout the Elizabethan era with the government only half-heartedly attempting to suppress it. If provoked the queen would restrain the pirates. When her envoy carrying a christening gift to the French court was attacked in the English Channel in 1573, she sent her fleet and troops into the West Country to round up hundreds of pirates, although most were eventually released.

In the West Country gentry with maritime connections were often the first to flout the law and engage in 'discriminating piracy' (as privateering was sometimes called). For them patriotism, plunder and Protestantism amalgamated to produce the motivation which fuelled the fires of

Sir John Hawkins (1532-95), from an early-17th-century engraving. His doomed trading voyage to the Spanish Main in 1568 did much to launch the undeclared naval war between Spain and England. He was knighted following the Spanish Armada campaign of 1588. (Mariners)

Queen Elizabeth I (1533-1603) was careful never to openly support her privateering captains before war with Spain broke out in 1585. Privately, she encouraged their actions and even provided financial support for raids against the Spanish Main. Engraving by unknown artist, *c.*1590.

Philip II of Spain (1527-98), the implacable enemy of Queen Elizabeth I. His 'invincible Armada' of 1588 was intended to topple the English monarch and replace her with a Catholic puppet. Etching by Jonas Suyerhoef, from *Duces Burgundiae, c.*1647. (MFMHS)

piracy and privateering. Often the same men, or their neighbours, held positions of local authority and were responsible for policing piracy in the west of England, the Bristol Channel, or along the south coast. In Southampton the mayor regularly released captured pirates, while the mayor of Dartmouth was fined when his open piratical connections were discovered by the Queen. Francis Drake came from a background of rural gentility in Devonshire, and was related to his mentor, John Hawkins. Hawkins himself was the son of a prominent Plymouth gentleman merchant and shipowner, with powerful local connections. Martin Frobisher was a Yorkshireman, but was raised in London in the house of his uncle, a knight who invested heavily in maritime ventures, including 'discriminating piracy'. Walter Raleigh was born into the Devonshire nobility, but became involved in privateering through investment and speculation. In other words, these 'sea dogs' emerged from a society which saw plundering on the high seas as an acceptable pursuit for gentlemen merchant adventurers and their actions were supported by their peers. As the officials who should have curtailed piracy often invested in piratical ventures themselves, or were related to the pirates, these activities were effectively legitimised. It was this large-scale participation of the southern gentry in 'discriminating piracy' which transformed the petty piracy in the English Channel of the mid-16th century into the transatlantic plundering of the Elizabethan 'sea dogs' from the 1570s.

Unless operating directly under the orders of the Queen, most expeditions conducted by the Elizabethan 'sea dogs' were speculative ventures, backed by investors or even companies and shareholders. The profit motive was paramount, particularly when the voyage or expedition combined trade with plunder. When, in 1560, Thomas White was returning to England from the Barbary coast of North Africa, for example, he came upon two Spanish ships carrying quicksilver. Although he was on a trading voyage, he attacked the ships, captured them, and took them back to London. The authorities in London ignored what was clearly an act of piracy, his investors reaped an immense profit and his crew were awarded prize money. Everyone benefited from White's action apart from the Spanish.

Even participants in peaceful ventures such the establishment of a colony in Virginia were tempted by this apparent free licence to plunder Spanish shipping, and Richard Grenville captured prizes sailing to and returning from a voyage to the Roanoake colony. One of the tricks used by the authorities to legitimise this kind of action was to issues 'Letters of Reprisal'. Unlike a privateering 'Letter of Marque' these were a form of redress against slights, real or imagined, caused by another country. In 1585, for example, a group of merchants who claimed the Spanish had impounded a cargo, were issued with a Letter of Reprisal allowing them to plunder an equivalent amount from Spanish shipping. The letter was issued to a specific ship, the 14-gun *Amity*, which was still harassing the Spanish nine years later!

Potential profit was a very powerful incentive and many vessels were fitted our as `privateers´ with the idea of financial gain in mind. The 'sea dogs' were also rarely short of manpower, at least when sailing on semi-legal plundering or trading ventures. From contemporary sources it is apparent that active privateering ships in the 1570s and 1580s carried around one man for every two tons of displacement. To the backers and commanders, large crews meant strong and efficient landing or boarding parties, and also allowed them to provide extra crews to man captured vessels. Almost exclusively, seamen on Elizabethan privateers received no wages, but instead received a portion of the plunder or cargo taken from their victims. Conditions on these ships were harsh, and death from starvation or disease was commonplace, especially on a long voyage. The handful of men who returned with John Hawkins after the failure of his 1568 expedition were almost dead from starvation and thirst, while numerous instances are recorded of crews being decimated by disease, particularly when operating in the Spanish Main. Both Drake and Hawkins died from fever, probably brought on by the 'bloody flux', or dysentery which flourished in the unsanitary conditions found on late-16th-century ships. A lack of basic hygiene simply provided a breeding ground for disease. The typical diet of an Elizabethan seaman was bread or ship's biscuit, salted beef, pork or fish, peasemeal, butter and cheese. Beer was readily available, and wine was issued to the crew when a Spanish vessel was captured. The lack of fresh fruit and vegetables led to scurvy, known as 'the plague of the sea' and food and beer rotted very quickly in the warm waters of the Caribbean. Local produce was sometimes purchased from the native population or from 'cimaroons' (or *cimarónes*), runaway slaves living on the fringes of the Spanish overseas empire. During Drake's voyage of circumnavigation, the expedition frequently purchased provisions from South Seas natives, which probably helped to prevent any major outbreak of disease among his crew.

Compared with the Queen's ships, discipline on Elizabethan privateers seems to have been extremely lax. Even hard taskmasters such as Drake found it difficult to control the crews. The execution of one of his captains, Thomas Doughty, in 1578 (charged with treason, mutiny and necromancy) may have been an attempt to enforce his will over a crew who were reluctant to sail through the Straits of Magellan into the Pacific, fearing that they would never be able to return home. With disorderly crews and frequent instances of drunkenness and fighting it is surprising the Elizabethan commanders accomplished what they did. The last recorded words of Sir George Carew who commanded the *Mary Rose* just before she sank in July 1545 were that he led 'the sort of knaves whom he could not rule'. This sounds similar to Thomas Cavendish's last words, when he called his sailors an 'insolent, mutinous company' in 1591, although the explorer and privateer was showing signs of extreme paranoia by the time he died. To experienced commanders such as Drake, the lack of discipline was a problem which could be overcome by dynamic leadership, but even he encountered problems when prize money was not forthcoming, or his sailors thought a venture was too dangerous.

Much has been written about the talents of the Elizabethan seamen, but they were probably no more skilled than other competent mariners from France or Spain. What set them apart was their desire for plunder, and therefore a share of prize money. As the size of privateering fleets and royal expeditions grew towards the close of the century, skilled seamen became more scarce, and an influx of landsmen meant that a deterioration in sailing ability and gunnery was inevitable. Incidentally, the reverse was true of the soldiers carried on board these expeditions. While the troops accompanying Drake in the mid 1580s were raw recruits, by the 1590s, experienced soldiers were vying for places on privateering expeditions, where plunder was more readily available than on the battlefields of the Spanish Netherlands. Service in privateers was miserable, but still considered preferable to manning one of the Queen's ships. As the commander Sir William Monson wrote, it is strange 'what misery such men will choose to endure in small ships of reprisal, though they be hopeless of gain, rather than serve Her Majesty, where their pay is certain, their diet plentiful and their labour not so great'. The prospect of a larger share of plunder was clearly a greater incentive than patriotism.

Little is known about the dress of the seamen who manned the privateers and warships of the Elizabethan era. Certain common features can be determined from contemporary depictions. Clothing worn by a seaman was usually simple. A tunic of leather or a worsted material was worn on its own, or with the addition of hose and a seaman's jacket. One-piece hose were worn on the *Mary Rose* (1545) and by Spanish seamen in the 1580s, so clearly remained popular throughout the period. Baggy woollen breeches similar to those worn on land appear to have been common, although Sir William Monson mentions seamen in petticoats or baggy canvas breeches. The petticoat or sailor's smock was a canvas or white duck skirt

LEFT **An Elizabethan English seaman. His baggy clothes were practical garments, and often coated in a tarring solution to provide some degree of waterproofing. Engraving by unknown artist, *c*.1580. (Author's collection)**

BELOW **This sleeveless leather jerkin was recovered from the wreck of the *Mary Rose*, and was typical of the dress of English seamen and sea soldiers throughout the late Tudor period. The slashed decoration allowed ease of movement. (*Mary Rose* Trust).**

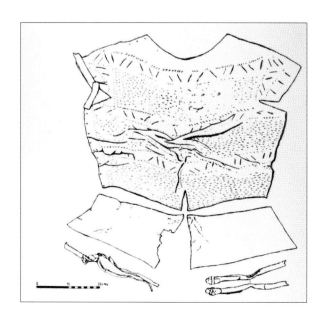

English seamen of the Elizabethan age. The character on the right wears a short seaman's jacket, but both are probably better dressed than any of the seamen found on board the ships of the Elizabethan 'sea dogs'. Frontispiece from Lucas Waghenaer, *The Mariners Mirrour,* (London, 1588). (NMM)

which reached below the knees, and was a common form of maritime wear from at least the 15th until the early-19th centuries. These could be worn as a simple skirt, or split into separate legs, in the style of modern culottes. Coarse shirts, frequently called 'undershirts' or 'stomachers', appear to have often been collarless, the neck closed by a simple drawstring. Seamen's jackets in the late-16th century were wool, and seldom reached below the waist. These tight-fitting garments ended in simple rolled collars and were fitted with tubular sleeves without cuffs. A rolled tube of wool at the shoulder is shown on the jacket of one of the seamen from the *Mariner's Mirror* (1588), and reflects civilian fashion. Both of the seamen in this illustration wear typical brown baggy woollen breeches and hose, but beyond that their clothing must be considered unusual, as one wears a decorated and padded coat, while both are shown wearing civilian collar ruffs. If worn, these embellishments may have been reserved for shore-going clothing by the more affluent gentlemen mariners, and there is no evidence that this was ever worn at sea. Archaeological evidence from the *Mary Rose* suggests that leather jerkins were also common. Another depiction of Elizabethan seamen shows a seaman in breeches, shirt, seaman's jacket and fur hat. Other forms of headgear in contemporary illustrations included berets, high or low-crowned felt hats, headscarves, woollen knitted caps and soft felt 'Phrygian' caps. Footwear recovered from the *Mary Rose* included leather shoes with a slash decoration, although most seamen would have gone barefoot on the high seas.

THE SPANISH MAIN AND ITS DEFENCES

The discovery of the Americas in 1492 launched Spain on a course of exploration and conquest which resulted in the establishment of her overseas 'empire'. The Treaty of Tordesillas (1494) gave Spain complete control of all newly discovered territories to the west of a mid-Atlantic line, leaving Portugal free to exploit everything to the east, including Brazil, Africa and India. The Spanish era of conquest, spearheaded by conquistadors such as Cortéz, Pisarro and de Soto, resulted in Spanish control over the Caribbean basin, Central America and the north and west coastlines of the South American continent. Spain's establishment of ports on the Pacific (then known as the 'South Sea') allowed her to found fresh colonies in the Philippines, giving her access to the lucrative spice, porcelain and silk markets of the Far East. The term, 'the Spanish Main', was originally coined to refer to the northern coastline of South America, but during the 16th century it came to refer to the entire Caribbean.

Following the capture of these new territories, the Spanish sought to colonise them, and to exploit the natural resources of the region. The main impetus behind the conquests of the conquistadors was the quest for plunder, and in the process of looting the Aztec and Incan empires the Spanish discovered that the region contained fantastic resources of

Map of the Spanish Main, showing the largest Spanish ports in the Caribbean Sea. Nombre de Dios (replaced by Porto Bello), Cartagena, Havana and Vera Cruz (off map) were the main ports used by the Spanish treasure fleets. (Author's collection)

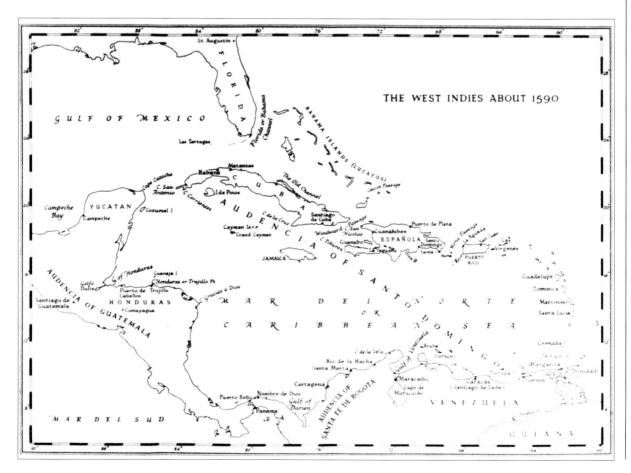

Potosi in Peru was the richest silver mine in the world during the late-16th century, producing more precious metals than the rest of the Spanish mines in the New World combined. Frontispiece of Zarate, *The Strange and Delectable History*, London, 1581. (Author's collection)

precious metals. Both Peru and Mexico were sources of silver, and the Potosi mine in southern Peru became the richest silver mine in the world by the mid-16th century. Gold was available in more modest quantities in the mountains of Venezuela, but the region also produced emeralds, while the pearl banks off Venezuela and Ecuador proved to be extremely productive. These valuable commodities were shipped to Spain using the annual Treasure Fleet (or *flota*) system. Each year a convoy left Seville in Spain, and crossed the Atlantic from the Cape Verde Islands to the southern Caribbean. Once in the Spanish Main the convoy split up, with smaller *flotas* going to different ports to collect the annual haul of treasure. The New Spain *flota* visited San Juan de Ulúa (later Vera Cruz), while the Tierre Firme *flota* went first to Nombre de Dios to collect the silver transported there from Peru, then on to Cartagena. Other smaller fleets formed part of the network, shipping silver from Lima to Panama, or spices from the Philippines to Mexico. The goods would be brought to the Caribbean treasure ports by mule train, then trans-shipped onto the *flotas*. All the *flotas* rendezvoused in Havana for the voyage back, the convoy route skirting Florida and the Bahamas before curving north and east past Bermuda and the Azores to reach Seville. This huge undertaking followed a timetable, and in its entirety formed the largest maritime trading system in the world. It

The Spaniards used native labour to mine for gold in Hispaniola and Venezuela, and silver in Mexico and Peru during the late-16th century. Engraving by Theodore de Bry, from *Americae pars quinta*, 1595. (MAS)

was also difficult to attack, as the treasure fleets themselves were well protected and only susceptible to large enemy fleets.

The weak links in this chain were the ports where the treasure was embarked. Nombre de Dios, San Juan de Ulúa, Havana, Cartagena and to a lesser extent Santo Domingo on Hispaniola were all major treasure ports, and all were captured at least once by English or French raiders. Following the Huguenot raids of the mid-16th century, the Spanish crown was sufficiently concerned about the vulnerability of the ports to begin a fortification programme, building stone fortresses, siting new shore batteries and training and equipping militiamen. Philip II appointed Pedro Menendez de Aviles, a Spanish nobleman and investor in maritime trade to reorganise the defences. Although he upgraded the defences of Havana and Cartagena as ordered, he also advocated a more aggressive defence, based around fleets of patrolling warships and galleys. Pedro Menendez also reorganised the *flota* system, making the convoys better prepared to defend themselves if attacked. In 1565 he was given command of an expedition of 30 ships and 2,000 soldiers, with orders to wipe out the French Huguenot settlement in Florida. Although a storm scattered his fleet during the Atlantic crossing, he continued with a small force, established a base at St Augustine and captured the French settlement. Another storm shipwrecked the French fleet based there, and the Spanish commander massacred the survivors on a Florida beach. His actions underlined the point that the Spanish would not tolerate any European incursion into their New World territories and they regarded everything west of the mid-Atlantic line drawn during the Treaty of Tordesillas, including anywhere in the Americas, as their territory. Three years later Hawkins was driven from San Juan de Ulúa, marking a fundamental shift in English attitudes towards the Spanish overseas empire. It developed from a potential source of trade and became a likely source of plunder, and 'sea dogs' such as Drake would ensure that there would be 'no peace beyond the line'.

Drake's raids from the early 1570s to the mid 1580s struck the Spanish Main at its most vulnerable. Since the impetus spearheaded by Pedro Menendez, little had been achieved, and a lack of funding and equipment meant that many of the smaller ports were virtually unprotected. Drake's seizure of Nombre de Dios in 1572 was achieved after the capture of a single battery and a skirmish with the local militia; only a tropical downpour and

The graceful hull lines of a Spanish treasure galleon of the 1580s. The sections emphasise the large cargo capacity of these vessels, which were designed to carry the wealth of the Americas home to Spain. From Diego Garcia de Palacio, *Instrución Nautica*, 1587. (PRO)

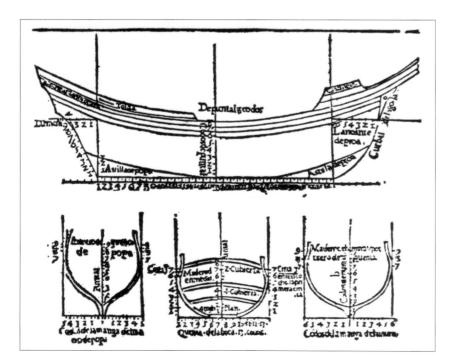

Most of the Spanish vessels which took part in the Spanish Armada campaign of 1588 were not custom-built galleons or warships. Instead, they resembled this well-armed merchant vessel. Engraving after Pieter Bruegel the elder, (c. 1529-1565). (NMM)

Drake's injury saved the Spanish from disaster. In his wider raids during 1585-86, he was able to land a large enough force so that he outnumbered the enemy, giving the English an inestimable advantage.

In the Old World, the union between Spain and Portugal in 1580 gave the Spanish the use of Lisbon, perhaps the best fortified anchorage on the Iberian Peninsula, along with a fleet of well-built warships and professional crews. The other Spanish ports of Cadiz, Seville, Vigo, El Ferrol and La Coruna were all reasonably well defended, and even if temporarily lost, over-whelming numbers of Spanish reinforcements were available to recapture the ports before they could be seriously damaged. The capture of Cadiz in 1596 showed how flawed this idea could be when the port was protected from Spanish counter-attack by the guns of the Anglo-Dutch fleet.

The Portuguese fleet was a valuable asset which had an important role to play in Philip II's new naval policy. In the 1560s, the Spanish had no permanent navy apart from the treasure *flotas* and a Mediterranean galley fleet. Pedro Menendez de Aviles argued that a small squadron was needed to protect the homeward-bound treasure *flotas* in Atlantic waters. In 1570 the *Armada Real de la Guarda de la Carrera de las Indias* was formed, and consisted of 12 small galleons of under 250 tons, commanded by Pedro Menendez himself. They were not part of a proper Atlantic fleet, but formed part of the treasure fleet system, and were rarely available for offensive actions.

During the 1580s ten large galleons were built, and these eventually formed part of the Castillian Squadron of the Armada of 1588. The Portuguese Atlantic fleet of nine galleons was a valuable addition to the *Armada Real*, but the fleet was still too small to be effective. During the Azores campaign of 1583, only three royal warships were available, and the Spanish had to revert to their traditional practice of hiring well-armed merchant vessels to form the backbone of their fleet. The same situation occurred during the Armada campaign of 1588, when of the 130 major ships which took part, only 27 were royal warships (the Portuguese and Castillian squadrons, plus eight galleys and galeasses). That Spain was able to rebuild her Atlantic fleet after her crushing losses in 1588 was a testimony to the resolve of Philip II. The Azores action of

1591 showed that within just three years, the Atlantic fleet was again capable of protecting Spain's treasure fleet against large-scale attacks.

The one great problem with the defence of the Spanish empire was that it was simply too difficult and expensive to protect. Although the principal New World ports were re-fortified during the 1590s, and Spanish treasure fleets sailed unmolested throughout the period, attacks by English and French 'sea dogs' highlighted the vulnerability of the ports to a sudden overwhelming attack. The English 'sea dogs' understood the concept of seapower expounded by Alfred Mahan 300 years later. Without control of the sea lanes and the principal ports, any empire which relied on a maritime lifeline for its financial wellbeing was extremely vulnerable, and invited attack.

THE ELIZABETHAN ART OF WAR

Arms and armour

A study of several of the accounts and inventories relating to Elizabethan 'sea dogs' reveals that at least on major expeditions, they were extremely well armed. A Spanish inventory of the weapons recovered from the ships of John Hawkins' expedition in 1568 is a prime example. The weapons captured at San Juan de Ulúa in 1568 included 89 muskets, 121 arquebuses, 16 *arquebus à croc* (oversized firearms used as rail guns), 105 half-pikes, halberds and other staff weapons, as well as dozens of swords, knives and daggers. A separate list exists describing the artillery and swivel guns captured in the fight. Although sources are contradictory, Hawkins probably sailed with around 405 men in his fleet. Given that about 230 escaped and some at least would have taken their weapons with them, this expedition was well supplied with weaponry, particularly small-arms. This reflects several accounts of the later amphibious landings conducted by Drake, when a large number of the landing parties carried firearms, although his men appear to have been less well equipped during his expeditions in the 1570s.

This reliance on firearms was reflected in the proportion of weapons issued to soldiers on the Queen's ships in 1588. As an example, Martin Frobisher's *Triumph* (1,100 tons) carried 300 sailors, 160 soldiers and

An English bronze demi-culverin recovered from the wreck of the *Mary Rose* together with its four-wheeled truck carriage. It was cast in Houndsditch, London for Henry VIII in 1537. It is typical of the guns carried by the English royal ships of the Elizabethan period, although the truck wheels were reduced in size by the 1580s. Drawing by Debbie Fulford. (*Mary Rose* Trust)

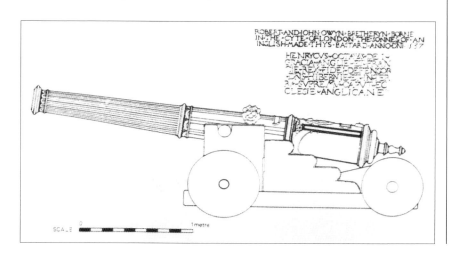

40 gunners, and 100 firearms were issued to the vessel before the Armada battles. This proportion of approximately two missile troops to every soldier equipped with a mêlée weapon is similar to the ratio found on the *Mary Rose*. Clearly, soldiers on board English ships were valued more for their firepower than for their use in a boarding action. As for the Spanish, a muster taken before the Armada sailed from Lisbon in 1588 recorded

that of the 18,937 soldiers in the fleet, less than half of them carried firearms (8,604, of which 1,000 were musketeers, the rest arquebusiers). Other archival sources indicate that the Spanish relied more heavily on shock troops than missile troops, and as late as 1622, shock troops (pikemen, halbardiers and swordsmen) outnumbered missile troops (armed with muskets and arquebuses) by a ratio of five to four, a ratio consistent with the Armada sources.

Firearms were undergoing a transition during the late-16th century. The arquebus was a hand-held matchlock weapon which fired a half-ounce ball. A late-16th-century musket was

a longer and far heavier weapon, which fired a ball weighing around one-and-a-half ounces. Muskets weighed around 20lbs apiece, and consequently had to be fired using a musket rest, or by leaning the weapon on the ship's rail. Unlike 17th century muskets, both Spanish and English weapons had an almost straight stock, meaning that the upper shoulder absorbed all of the weapon's considerable recoil. Surviving arquebuses of the period had a drooping, downward-curved stock, allowing the weapon to be couched under the armpit. The effective range of the musket has been placed at 80-90 yards, and the arquebus at 50-60 yards, with a rate of fire of approximately one round per minute. Crossbows were also carried, and have been found on Spanish wrecks of the 1550s (Padre Island, Texas) and 1560s, (St Johns, Bahamas) although inventories list them as being carried by both English and Spanish warships as late as the Armada campaign of 1588.

Shock (or close-combat) troops used swords or half-pikes on board, and reserved halberds and full 16-18ft pikes for engagements on land. Pikemen were regarded as elite troops by Spanish warships, held 'in so great esteem that they seldom commit them but to gentlemen'. The wreck of an Elizabethan vessel off Alderney in the 1580s produced the remains of bills, and while tradition suggests that this was a predominantly English weapon, bills were also found on a Spanish wreck in the Bahamas dated 1564, so evidently a variety of staff weapons was carried by both sides. Other edged weapons included rapiers, worn by soldiers and officers, and often used in conjunction with a main-gauche (a form of left-handed dagger). A precursor of the cutlass was the hanger, which was primarily a hunting sword, but was widely used at sea; the carrying of a dagger or long knife was commonplace.

Pictorial and documentary sources indicate that Elizabethan mariners wore armour, at least when they ventured ashore. Often this was limited to a simple steel morion or *cabacet*, although close-combat soldiers on both Spanish or English warships wore back and breast plates and even tassets. More commonly, English mariners on land wore padded leather or cotton jerkins for protection, although 'brigandines' (padded jackets incorporating sewn-in metal protective plates) can be seen in several contemporary illustrations of landing parties. It seems that mariners on an Elizabethan privateer were equipped with sufficient weapons and armour to give the appearance of well-armed regular soldiers when they participated in amphibious raids. The soldiers carried on royal vessels were probably even better equipped and protected, and certainly better trained and disciplined. As for the Spanish, their soldiers were considered the best in Europe, and at least during the Spanish Armada campaign, their presence made any attempt at boarding a Spanish vessel virtually inconceivable to their English opponents.

Amphibious tactics

The amphibious raids conducted against Spanish towns during the Elizabethan era were a novelty outside the Mediterranean, where coastal raiding was commonplace during the interminable wars between Muslims and Christians. The development of a tactical doctrine can be demonstrated by examining three raids conducted by Francis Drake.

In 1572 he led a force of 74 troops in an attack on Nombre de Dios; 24 men were armed with pikes and spears, 40 with arquebuses and

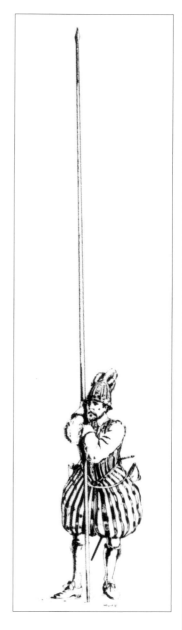

A reconstruction of a Spanish sea soldier pikeman of 1588, based on artefacts recovered from *La Trinidad Valencera*. Although this soldier formed part of the troops intended to land in England, the Spanish used pikemen on board their ships, although 'half-pikes' and other staff weapons were more suitable for use on board ship than the standard 18ft pike. Drawing by Ian Lowe. (Author's collection, from Martin)

crossbows, six with a sword and shield and there was a command party of four drummers and trumpeters. They approached the harbour in three pinnaces and a shallop at dawn, and Drake realised that against a more numerous enemy, his only chance of success was to keep the Spaniards off-balance. He captured a six gun battery which defended the harbour and posted 12 men to guard it and the boats. He led the rest towards the town, splitting off a force of 18 men to approach the town from the inland road. Drake led the rest of his men straight towards the town centre, where church bells were sounding the alarm. A body of town militia commanded by the mayor (*alcalde*), Antonio Juarez, formed up in the central square and blocked Drake's path. A firefight ensued, and although the English suffered few casualties, Drake was wounded. The militia was routed when the flanking party arrived in the square behind them, and Drake held the town centre. At the Governor's house he found a strongroom filled with silver bars, but he wanted more. Drake knew that the King's warehouse on the waterfront held gold, so he pushed on through the town, just as a sudden tropical downpour lashed the area. With their gunpowder and crossbow strings useless, and Drake faint from loss of blood, the English seamen decided to withdraw back to their boats, leaving the town and the treasure to be recaptured by the Spaniards. Although a failure, the raid showed that Drake relied on surprise and momentum to overcome the Spaniards' numerical advantage.

Drake's expedition of 1585 was an altogether grander venture than his previous raids, and his fleet carried 12 companies of soldiers commanded by Christopher Carleill. They were raw recruits, but were armed and equipped with the latest muskets, arquebuses and pikes. On 17 November 1585 Carleill landed to the east of the town of Santiago in the Cape Verde Islands. Although the town was protected by forts and earthworks containing at least 50 guns, the defences were known to be in poor repair, and the garrison was weak. One thousand soldiers stormed the town as Drake's ships bombarded the defences from the sea, and the garrison fled without firing a shot. Drake used reconnaissance (the landward defences were known to be weak on the eastern side of the town) and naval gunfire support to good effect, as well as relying on professional (albeit inexperienced) soldiers to undertake the amphibious landing. The attack may well have been launched to give the recruits a baptism of fire before they attacked the larger cities of the Spanish Main.

The same basic plan was followed when Drake assaulted Santo Domingo on New Year's Day, 1586. Carleill led his men in a land assault, while Drake bombarded the city from the sea. A Spanish force of horse and foot sent to attack the landing party was driven off, but as the English approached the city the Spanish drove a herd of cattle into their ranks. This disruptive tactic was later used against Henry Morgan during his attack

Thomas Cavendish (1560-1592) took part in the Virginia venture of 1585 before undertaking a voyage of circumnavigation in 1587. En route he captured a Spanish Manila galleon carrying treasure from the Philippines to Mexico. Engraving by an unknown artist, early-17th century. (Mariners)

Francis Drake's attack on Cartagena, 1586. This well planned and executed attack was perhaps the most successful of Drake's raids on the treasure cities of the Spanish Main. Engraving by Theodore de Bry, c.1590. (MFMHS)

on Panama in 1671, and in both cases it backfired. The cattle simply ran the wrong way and disrupted the defenders instead of the attackers. Carleill's men drove the disorganised Spaniards ahead of them and captured the city.

Cartagena was a much stronger city, defended by stone walls, a fort and boom guarding the entrance to the anchorage, with a cordon of earthworks protecting the approaches to the city. A squadron of three galleys also protected the inner harbour. A spit of land, the 'Caretta', separated the port's outer anchorage and inner harbour from the sea, and Carleill's 1,000 men were landed on the spit under cover of darkness, out of sight from the fort on one side and the city on the other. Drake pinned the rest of the defenders down by feinting an attack on the main anchorage. The city was defended by 600 Spanish militia and 400 Indian allies, the latter armed with bows and poisoned arrows, but these were scattered around the perimeter of the city, while Carleill's soldiers were concentrated. The English stormed the barricade blocking Caretta just outside the town, driving off the militia and Indians after a sharp engagement. This time it was the Spanish who provided gunnery support from their galleys, although in the dark they fired high and caused negligible casualties. The Spanish withdrew to barricades in the city itself, but their morale was broken, and the English drove them from the town. As raw troops were used on both sides, the arbiter of victory was morale, and the English stuck to a simple plan and were confident of victory.

In all these engagements, the keys to English success were concentration of force, pinning down the defenders by a feint attack and the maintenance of the tactical initiative. Drake learned from his failure in Nombre de Dios, and when given the manpower and weaponry to achieve his objectives, his tactical skills ensured victory.

Naval Gunnery

Very little is known about gunnery procedures during the period, even on land, but a combination of archaeological and historical evidence provides useful clues. The methods of firing were similar on both land and sea, although naval gunnery had certain unique qualities. First, gunports were small during the latter half of the 16th century, the smallest main ports on the *Mary Rose* measuring only 2ft across. This meant that it was difficult to train the guns, a restriction amplified by the often cramped space on the gun deck and the requirement to secure the pieces to the side of the ship. If this was a problem for

This section of a bronze demi-culverin (*medio-culebrina*) cast with an off-centre bore. A poorly-cast gun would be extremely dangerous to fire. Recovered from the wreck of the Spanish Armada vessel *El Gran Grifon*, wrecked off Fair Isle off the north of Scotland. (Dr. Colin Martin)

English truck-wheeled carriages which could protrude further through the gunport, it was far worse for the two-wheeled carriages favoured by the Spanish. Sir William Monson writing about Spanish carriages during the 1560s stated that '...the pieces, in lying, cannot be traversed from side to side, but must be shot off directly forward as they lie'. If they could not be trained, at least they could be elevated or depressed, which was not really an important consideration on a rolling ship. In his artillery treatise of 1587, Sir William Bourne emphasised the importance of sighting artillery, but admitted that scientific calculations were difficult to apply at sea. Instead, he proposed that 'firing on the roll' was the solution; waiting for the downward roll of the ship to ensure that the shot did not overshoot the enemy, and preferably to fire when the enemy was rising on the swell, so her hull would be exposed below the waterline. Archaeological evidence also suggests that at least in hostile waters, guns were kept loaded, even when they were not in use.

Gun crews were smaller than in later periods. Sir Walter Raleigh stated that late-16th-century gun crews usually consisted of four men, while early-17th century sources list crews numbering between two and five men, depending on the size of the gun. The *Anthony Roll* of 1546 gives the organisation of late Tudor crews, with the *Mary Rose* (as an example) carrying 30 heavy guns, 30 gunners, 185 soldiers and 200 mariners. This procedure continued throughout the Elizabethan period, although the number of soldiers was gradually decreased during the last half of the 16th century. It is clear that one gunner was allocated to each gun, but if a full gun crew was supplied from the ranks of the soldiers and mariners, firing and reloading would involve most of the ship's complement, apart from archers, arquebusiers, swivel gun crews and a handful of sailors to handle the ship.

This bronze 'saker' (*sacre*) of Italian origin was recovered from the Spanish Armada vessel *Juliana*, wrecked off Streedagh Strand on the west coast of Ireland. It was subjected to an accident which blew out a section of the gun, demonstrating that some of the Armada weaponry was of dubious quality. (Dr. Colin Martin)

This organisation is echoed in Spanish sources. During the Armada campaign, gun crews consisted of a gunner and six soldiers. Once the gun was loaded the soldiers picked up their weapons and prepared to fight a boarding action. From all this it is evident that if more than one salvo was fired, reloading would involve a significant drop in the vessel's ability to fight a boarding action. In other words, it was one or the other, boarding or broadsides, but not both. It has been suggested that before a ship engaged in combat the captain would decide what sort of engagement he planned to fight, and would organise his crews accordingly.

Once a gun was fired, it had to be reloaded in what were often very cramped conditions. Wrought-iron breech-loading guns were carried on Spanish armed merchant ships at least until the 1590s, although they were considered obsolete by other maritime powers. These guns could be easily reloaded by replacing the powder chamber with another containing a fresh charge, and swivel guns were reloaded in the same manner, ensuring a rapid rate of fire. They were limited to close-range fire, and the preferable alternative was to use longer–range and more powerful muzzle-loading pieces which were reloaded by performing outboard or inboard loading. Inboard was the standard method in later centuries, but the cramped nature of Elizabethan warships often made this impossible, and one of the *Mary Rose* pieces could not be reloaded inboard because there was a bulkhead directly behind the gun. After firing, the gun had to be unlashed from the ship's side, then hauled backwards and loaded from within the safety of the hull. Outboard loading involved the loader climbing outside the hull, either through a gunport or down from the weatherdeck. The gunner would then sit astride the gun to clean and load the piece. The practice continued into the 1620s, but it was a hazardous and difficult undertaking.

An analysis of the artillery shot recovered from Spanish Armada wrecks provides an invaluable insight into Spanish gunnery during the campaign of 1588. Archival research recorded what quantities were issued when the various ships sailed. While almost no swivel gun or wrought-iron breech-loading ammunition was recovered, most of the shot issued for the larger guns was still carried on board when the ship went down. This indicated that the larger the gun, the less often it was fired during the Armada battles. It is imagined that much of the close-range firing was performed during the Battle of Gravelines, the last engagement of the campaign. The problems of reloading large demi-culverins on two-wheeled carriages were so acute that the pieces were rarely fired, in some cases only one or two shots being fired each day from the biggest guns. The short-range breech-loaders and swivels were easier to reload, and consequently were used more. Another factor was the reliability of guns. From a sample of around two dozen Spanish Armada bronze guns, two show significant structural

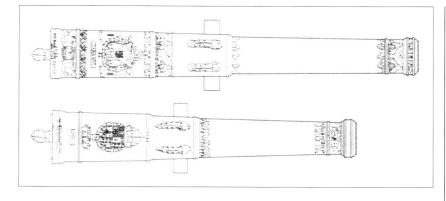

Spanish artillery pieces carried by vessels involved in the Spanish Armada.

ABOVE **A full cannon (*cañon de batir*) with a 7in bore (10ft 8in long) based on a contemporary drawing. The gun was cast for Charles V in Augsburg, Germany in 1538.**

BELOW **Another 7in cannon recovered from the wreck of *La Trinidad Valencera* in 1987. It is 8ft 8in long, and was cast in Mechelin, Belgium for Philip II in 1556. (Dr. Colin Martin)**

A Spanish artillery piece mounted on a sea carriage, c.1590. During the period, the Spanish mounted their guns on two-wheeled carriages which were less well suited to use on board ships than the carriages employed by their adversaries. (Archivo General de Simancas, Valladolid)

defects, and one of these apparently blew a chunk out of its barrel when it was being fired. The Spanish usually elected to fight a boarding action, and their guns were designed to fire once prior to boarding. If reloading them would disrupt the ship's preparedness for fighting a boarding action, and if some of the guns were considered unreliable, then the lack of Spanish enthusiasm for fighting a gunnery action is understandable.

English bronze and even cast-iron guns were considered of high quality, and English sailors using four-wheeled truck carriages could rely on their equipment and skill to maintain a constant fire, limited only by the available supplies of powder and shot. The fact that the English were running out of ammunition in the middle of the Armada campaign and the Spanish were not is clear evidence of the different gunnery methods the opponents relied on to win the battle.

Naval warfare

By the mid-16th century, artillery had established itself as a necessary tool in naval warfare. It was still not the dominant weapon type, but instead formed part of an integrated range of weaponry. Evidence from the warship *Mary Rose* which sank in Portsmouth harbour in 1545 emphasises this integrated approach. She carried a mixture of ordnance, including large bronze pieces as well as wrought-iron breech-loading guns mounted on wooden beds. Swivel guns mounted on the ships rail provided close-range firepower, augmented by 'hackbutts' and 'arquebuses'. On board, archers outnumbered firearm-carrying infantry, while bills and other staff weapons were provided for use during a boarding action. To complete the array, firepots and other incendiary weapons were carried in limited numbers. The *Mary Rose* was designed primarily as a platform for close-range weaponry, and her ability to engage in a protracted artillery duel was minimal.

Naval tactics had developed by the middle of the century to take advantage of the revolution created by ship-borne artillery. Two theories had emerged, the more traditional based around using the ship as an integrated weapon and favouring boarding actions; the other, more revolutionary notion advocated using the artillery carried on board as the primary offensive weapon. The English, and to a lesser extent the Dutch and the French took full advantage of the introduction of reliable artillery to rethink their approach to naval warfare. Although circumstance largely dictated which approach was used, these nations tended to develop a doctrine based around the use of artillery as an offensive weapon. In short, the Spanish relied on boarding to win a sea battle, while their enemies preferred to keep their distance and rely on gunnery to win the fight.

During the Armada campaign, soldiers loaded the Spanish guns, and then a solitary gunner was left to man the artillery piece while the soldiers armed themselves with boarding weapons. The role of the soldiers and the swivel gunners was to engage enemy boarding parties immediately before two ships locked in combat. Artillery was fired one salvo at the same time, partly to sweep the decks of the enemy and partly to pound the forecastle and sterncastles of the enemy vessel, creating a breach through which assault parties could storm the enemy ship. This was the same tactic used in the days of the *Mary Rose* over 40 years earlier, and made no concessions to recent developments in gunnery. Spanish

A 16th century representation of an incendiary firepot (*alcancia*). These weapons were thrown in a manner similar to modern hand grenades, and were used by all the maritime powers of the late-16th century. Engraving from Cyprian Lucar, *Tartaglia's Colloquies and Lucar's Appendix*, London, 1588. (Royal Armouries, HM Tower of London)

vessels did not rely on this form of combat to the exclusion of gunnery, and evidence from engagements as early as 1568 suggest that the Spanish could perform long-range fire if they chose to. During the attack on Filipo Strozzi's French fleet in the Azores in 1582, the Spaniards used gunnery to defeat their opponent, and tended to employ tactics developed by the galley fleets of the Mediterranean. During the Elizabethan period, they were clearly still writing the tactical manuals, and innovation and organisation were often more important than tactical doctrine.

The big advantage that the English enjoyed over the Spanish was that for the most part they used a four-wheeled gun carriage. It allowed the gun to be run up closer to the gun port, making the piece easier to aim or to traverse. Also, the gun's weight was distributed between four points, each of them a small truck wheel. The Spanish relied on two-wheeled carriages which resembled land guns, but with solid or almost solid wheels. On some vessels, these wheels could be as much as three feet high, making the piece unwieldy, and also distributing the weight onto three points (two wheels and a trail). Another significant innovation was that the English developed a simple system of blocks, ropes and tackles which allowed the guns to be pulled inboard by their own recoil, reloaded and then run out again with the minimum amount of effort. The same system was refined until it became the standard form of mounting and firing naval guns in the 17th century. By contrast, archaeological and historical evidence suggests that the Spanish, who lashed their guns to the hulls of their ships, had to untie the ropes, and then physically manhandle them inboard in order to

The Florentine nobleman Filippo Strozzi commanded a French fleet which attempted to capture the Azores from the Spanish. In July 1582 he was defeated and killed in a fleet action against a Spanish squadron led by the Marquis de Santa Cruz. (Bibliothèque Nationale, Paris)

Reconstruction of the gun deck of the *Mary Rose* showing the range of ordnance carried. The two wrought-iron breech-loading guns (known as 'port pieces' or 'murderers') were considered obsolete by the 1580s, although several Spanish armed merchant vessels carried them during the Armada campaign of 1588. (*Mary Rose* Trust)

In this late-16th-century engraving by an unknown artist, an assailant is depicted nailing firepots to the hull of an enemy vessel. The dangers involved in any enterprise involving incendiary weapons at sea are self-evident. (Biblioteca Nacional, Madrid)

Another incendiary weapon was the fire lance (*bomba*), a form of offensive firework on a stick which could be thrust into the faces of the enemy during a boarding action. Engraving from Cyprian Lucar, *Tartaglia's Colloquies and Lucar's Appendix*, London, 1588. (Royal Armouries, HM Tower of London)

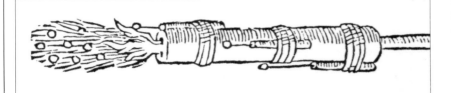

reload. Another advantage of the truck carriage was space. While a typical English carriage was smaller than the gun itself, many Spanish carriages had long trails, making the gun and carriage a lengthy and unwieldy addition to an already crowded gundeck. During the Armada celebrations of 1988, two replicas were made and given to trained naval crews to operate. It was found that the same gun mounted on a replica Spanish carriage took about ten to 15 minutes to reload compared to the five minutes when mounted on the replica truck carriage. The four-wheeled truck carriage was present on the *Mary Rose* when she sank in 1545, so it was far from a new invention in 1588. The Spanish simply ignored the innovation, and continued to ignore it well into the 17th century. The remains of two-wheeled naval carriages were recovered from the wreck of the Spanish treasure galleon *Nuestra Señora de Atocha*, which wrecked in 1622.

Once these guns were fired, they had to be reloaded. The physical problems have already been discussed, but reloading had tactical implications as well. In a number of contemporary accounts of gunnery actions, vessels are said to have fired a broadside, then turned, presenting their bow or stern guns to the enemy and fired the other broadside after continuing to turn. This derived from the notion that in order to reload in safety, a ship would have to retire to a safe distance from the enemy, or alternatively, reload on the disengaged side while firing the rest of its armament at the enemy. The tactic used was similar to the *carracole*, a contemporary cavalry evolution, where a column of riders took turns to fire at the enemy, retiring to the rear rank to reload. It was not uncommon for warships to fight an enemy by sailing in a 'figure of eight', alternately firing each part of its heavy armament at the enemy while reloading on the disengaged side. These tactics were a far cry from the 'line of battle' actions fought from the late-17th century onwards.

The greatest sea battle of the century between rival fleets of sailing ships was fought at the end of the Spanish Armada campaign of 1588. The engagement at Gravelines was a loose mêlée, and was the exception rather than the rule, but the Armada campaign taken in its entirety demonstrates the two rival doctrines and their drawbacks. For the entire campaign, the Spanish maintained a dense formation, where each ship was supported by several others. In a number of occasions during the progress up the English

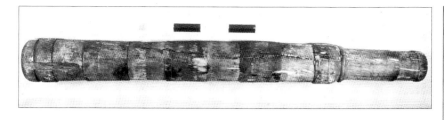

Channel the Spanish broke the formation to rescue ships which had fallen behind, or to attack isolated groups of English ships. The English were unable to make any impression on the dense Armada formation. Gunnery alone seemed unable to break up an enemy fleet. It was only when the formation was broken that the English were able to gain a tactical advantage over their adversaries, and with their faster vessels and efficient artillery were able to concentrate on individual Spanish ships. Throughout the campaign the Spanish relied on their 'boarding action' tactic, but the English simply stayed out of the way, although often the two fleets came close enough to fire arquebuses at each other. The successes of many of the Elizabethan 'sea dogs' arose from their ability to understand the tactical problems facing both themselves and their opponents, and their skill in adapting these limitations to their advantage.

A fire lance (bomba) recovered from the wreck of the Spanish Armada vessel La Trinidad Valencera after the removal of its slowmatch bindings. The weapon was just over two feet long, and was mounted on the end of a far longer stick. (Dr. Colin Martin)

Naval Ordnance
Both sides carried similar ordnance, mainly bronze guns, and conformed to the very general contemporary typology shown below.

Although most of these pieces were bronze, the English had experimented with the production of cheaper and equally efficient cast iron guns from the mid 1550s, which became increasingly common as the century progressed. While royal English warships continued to rely on bronze guns, possibly as many as half of the ordnance carried on armed merchantmen were iron guns. The Spanish also used bronze guns, but during the Elizabethan period they lacked the metallurgical technology required to produce their own reliable cast iron pieces. Evidence from Armada wrecks also suggests some of the hastily-cast bronze guns carried on Armada ships had flaws which would make them prone to bursting if fired.

In one study, Dr Colin Martin divided the artillery carried on the ships of the Spanish Armada into five distinct groups: *cañones* (cannons),

Table of types of late-16th-century artillery, selected from *William Bourne, The Arte of Shooting in great Ordnaunce*

	Calibre	Length	Weight	Shot Weight
Double Cannon	8in.	12ft	7,500lb	64lb
Demi-Cannon	6½in.	10-11ft	5,500lb	33lb
Culverin	5½in.	12ft	4,500lb	17lb
Demi-Culverin	4½in.	10ft	2,700lb	10¾lb
Saker	3¾in.	8-9ft	1,500lb	6lb
Minion	3¼in.	8ft	900lb	3lb
Falcon	2¾in.	7ft	700-750lb	2½lb
Falconet	2¼in.	5-6ft	360-400lb	1⅛lb

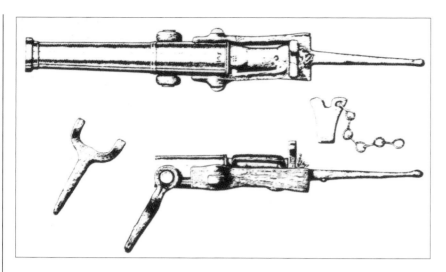

This large, breech-loading bronze swivel gun with wrought-iron fittings was recovered from the wreck of the Spanish Armada vessel *La Trinidad Valencera*. Called a '*pedrero*' or '*verso*' by the Spanish, it is typical of the close-range smaller guns carried on board ships of all nationalities during the Elizabethan period. (Dr. Colin Martin)

pedreros (stone-shotted guns), *culebrinas* (culverins), 'man-killers' and 'obsolescent guns'. In both nation's ships, cannons were heavy pieces, with a small ratio of length to calibre. Culverins were lighter and longer, and the culverin family included 'sakers', 'minions' 'falcons' and 'falconets'. *Pedreros* (or 'perriers' in English) were short-barrelled guns with a small powder chamber which fired stone shot. Both sides used 'man-killing' pieces, often mounted on the ship's rails on swivel mounts. The Spanish called these swivel guns *esmeriles* or *versos*, while the English called them 'bases'. They fired a charge of scrap metal or a clump of musket balls at point-blank range. Martin's 'obsolescent' guns were almost exclusively carried on Spanish armed merchantmen in small numbers. Wrought-iron breech-loading pieces known as *lombardas* or *bombardettas*, they were called 'port-pieces' or 'murderers' by the English. They were carried on the *Mary Rose* when she sank in 1545, but by 1588 their poor range and velocity made them obsolete. Given the Spanish tactical doctrine of firing at point-blank range prior to boarding the enemy, they would still have been relatively effective if the English ships had attempted to come close enough. The principal Spanish gun types are listed below, together with their equivalent name in English.

Spanish	English
Cañon de Batir	Double Cannon
Cañon	Demi-Cannon
Culebrina	Culverin
Media Culebrina	Demi-Culverin
Sacre	Saker
Medio sacre	Minion
Media Falconeta	Falcon
Falcon	Falconet

THE 'SEA DOGS' IN ACTION

This section will trace the outlines of the principal raids and campaigns undertaken by the Elizabethan 'sea dogs'. Rather than provide a detailed historic account of the period, the aim is to illustrate the range of methods used by the 'sea dogs' to fight the Spanish, and to demonstrate a number of military and naval trends which emerged during the conflict. In a period when both land and sea warfare was undergoing something of a revolution, the protagonists often had to develop new doctrines in order to exploit the military tools they had at their disposal.

The genius of men like Drake and Raleigh was their skill in mastering a situation, whether on land or sea, in a small raid or in a major sea battle. Military ability was not always enough to win a particular engagement without a prodigious degree of good fortune, and in this period, fortune did not always favour the brave.

The French Huguenot scourge

In the spring of 1523, a squadron of three Spanish ships lay off the south-west corner of Portugal on the last leg of their journey from Havana to Seville. They carried plunder looted from Mexico by Cortéz, a tribute to the Hapsburg Spanish

French Huguenot raiders sacking a Spanish settlement on the coast of Cuba, c.1545. During the 1540s, both Havana and Santiago were attacked and plundered. Hand-coloured engraving by Theodore de Bry, 1590. (MAS)

king, Charles V. The look-outs spotted five strange sails, and within hours two of the three Spanish treasure ships were overhauled, fired on and captured. Their assailants were French 'corsairs' led by Jean Fleury (or Florin), and his act of piracy would have serious repercussions. For the first time, other European powers became aware of the fortune which Spain was extorting from her New World possessions. Within a decade, dozens of other French corsairs would emerge, intent on plundering what was clearly the richest source of treasure in the world, and the French monarch, Francis I openly encouraged any action which would hurt his Hapsburg rival. In late 1527 Fleury was captured by the Spanish and executed, but other corsairs willingly took his place.

In 1527 Spanish ships were attacked off Brazil, and in 1533 a French corsair captured a homeward-bound treasure ship, forcing the Spanish to institute a convoy system for the first time. Peace between Spain and France in 1529 did little to stop the attacks, and when war erupted again in 1536, the French crown actively encouraged privateers. As with the later English 'sea dogs', wartime privateers simply became pirates in peacetime, although as their victim was always the Spanish, little or no action was taken against them. In 1540 a settlement on Puerto Rico was sacked by corsairs, and similar raids continued for a decade against the smaller Caribbean ports, such as Margarita, Santa Marta and even Cartagena. Although the Treaty of Crépy (1544) ended the Hapsburg-Valois conflict between Spain and France, religion as well as avarice became an important factor, and growing numbers of Protestant French Huguenot raiders used religious differences with the Catholic Spanish as an excuse for continuing the policy of plundering the Spanish Main.

25

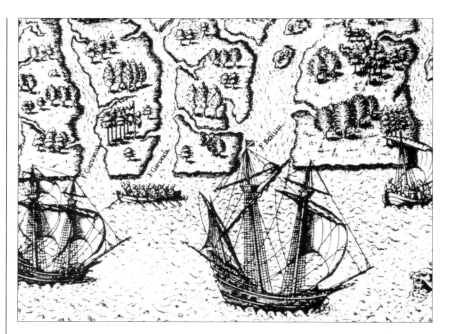

The French Huguenot ships of Jean Ribault off the east coast of Florida. His threat to the Spanish ended when his privateering squadron was wrecked in a hurricane in 1565. The Spanish massacred all the sailors who survived. Engraving by Theodore de Bry, c.1590. (MAS)

Another war in 1552 prompted a fresh wave of attacks. The corsair Antoine Alphonse was killed during an assault on Tenerife in November 1552, but the rest of the Canary Islands were devastated by Huguenot attacks, the principal raider being known as François Le Clerk, or `Jambe-de-Bois' ('Peg-Leg'). This fresh on-slaught caught the Spanish ports in the new world largely unprepared, and for the next seven years the French had virtually a free reign of the Spanish Main. In 1553, corsairs destroyed the Spanish settlements on the northern coast of Hispaniola, forcing the colonists to abandon most of the island. In the following year Santiago de Cuba was captured and sacked, along with a string of smaller Spanish settlements in Cuba. On 10 July 1555 a French squadron arrived off Havana, led by Jaques de Sores, a Huguenot corsair from La Rochelle. The Governor and most of the population fled inland leaving the small garrison in the fort guarding the town to fend for itself. The Spanish troops surrendered after a day, but the fort (and most of the town) contained little of value. The raiders amused themselves by desecrating churches in the settlement, and killing everyone they captured, and then repeating the performance in the surrounding countryside. Repulsing a Spanish counter-attack, de Sores ordered the town to be burned before he sailed away. Similar raids on Campeche in Mexico and Trujillo in Honduras, as well as attacks on Spanish shipping throughout the Caribbean brought the flow of New World treasure to a standstill.

During the mid-1560s, a French Huguenot settlement was established at Fort Caroline, near the modern city of Jacksonville, Florida. The Spanish feared it could be used as a base from which to attack the Spanish Main, and raised a force to destroy the interlopers and their colony. The Spanish force was commanded by Pedro Menendez de Aviles, a skilled soldier and colonial administrator. Menendez destroyed Fort Caroline in a land attack, but Ribault and his squadron were at sea, searching for Menendez. A hurricane decimated the French fleet, and Ribault and the survivors were cast ashore south of the new Spanish settlement of St Augustine. Menendez raced south and massacred the castaways, sparing only five ships' boys. This act of religious genocide marked the end of the large-scale French incursions. A religious civil war at home in France kept the Huguenot corsairs occupied at home, and the Spanish were granted a brief respite before a new group of English raiders descended on their Caribbean colonies.

The first English interloper

The Reformation brought about a strategic shift in European alliances. England was traditionally a staunch ally of the Hapsburgs, united against the common enemy, France. Following Henry VIII's break with Rome, relations deteriorated steadily, and after Elizabeth I's succession in 1558, Spain and England had become staunch religious and political enemies. Open conflict between the two nations was almost inevitable. It was in this atmosphere of religious hostility that the first English interloper ventured into the Caribbean, but unlike the French he sought to trade rather than to attack Spanish settlements.

John Hawkins was a Plymouth merchant and slave trader who transported a cargo of 300 slaves from West Africa to the Spanish Main. Although trade with interlopers was forbidden by the Spanish authorities, Hawkins hoped that many local governors would turn a blind eye to business with the English. He arrived off Hispaniola in early 1563 and connived with a local Spanish army officer to sell all of his slaves. This first voyage to the Spanish Main was a resounding financial success, making Hawkins the richest man in Plymouth. The investors who supported his plans for a second voyage included the Queen, who even leased him a ship, the aged *Jesus of Lubeck*, a 700-ton warship. This time the Spaniards were more reluctant to deal with him, but after being turned away from Margarita, Hawkins sold his human cargo at Borburata in Venezuela, and Rio Hatcha in Colombia after threatening to turn his guns on the towns if the local authorities refused to trade with him. This may have been an excuse contrived by both parties to justify the trade to the Spanish government if they found out about it. Hawkins returned to Plymouth in late 1565 with even greater profits than before, prompting the Spanish ambassador to lodge an official complaint at court. A third voyage was planned.

In early October 1567, Hawkins sailed for the West African coast in the *Jesus*, accompanied by another royal ship, the *Minion*, and four smaller vessels, plus a pinnace (large launch). The African part of the voyage was a disaster. An initial and unsuccessful slaving raid near Cape Verde left eight sailors dead, killed by poisoned arrows. Other raids produced a mere handful of captives until Hawkins reached Sierra Leone. There he allied himself with two local chieftains who wanted to attack a rival town. In a bitterly fought struggle Hawkins and his allies captured the town of Conga and the English slave decks were filled.

By early June 1568 the English expedition had reached the Caribbean. A hostile welcome at Rio Hatcha resulted in a skirmish with the local garrison, and after seizing the town, Hawkins was forced to withdraw with little profit to show for his efforts. At Santa Marta the governor arranged to put up a token resistance before being 'forced' to trade with the interlopers. The next port was Cartagena, and when the

Sir John Hawkins was a key figure in the development of the Elizabethan navy. As its treasurer, his integrity has been questioned, although as a naval commander he displayed singular skill and courage. Oil on panel. English school, dated 1581. (NMM)

governor refused to have anything to do with Hawkins, he retaliated by bombarding the batteries defending the port. It was clear that the Spanish authorities had clamped down on trading with Hawkins after his first two voyages. He sailed north, but in September his fleet encountered a hurricane off the western tip of Cuba. Although none of his ships were lost, they were all damaged, so Hawkins decided to put into the Spanish port of San Juan de Ulúa for repairs. San Juan was the port for the Mexican coastal city of Vera Cruz, where Mexico's silver was collected by the annual treasure fleets. The English fleet entered the harbour at dawn under false colours on 16 September 1569, and seized the port's defences before the small garrison could react. It appeared that Hawkins would be able to repair his ships in relative security, but the situation drastically altered the following morning. The treasure fleet arrived, 12 ships commanded by Admiral Francisco Luján. The Spanish sent assurances that they would leave the English in peace, and Hawkins allowed them to dock next to his own ships. The uneasy peace was shattered on the morning of 23 September when the Spaniards launched a surprise attack on the interlopers.

The English garrison on San Juan de Ulúa was quickly overrun, and Hawkins pulled his ships away from the dock. The Spaniards promptly manned the shore batteries and a prolonged artillery duel followed, with the English getting much the worst of the exchange. Hawkins had no option but to try to run through the gauntlet (and the unmarked offshore reefs) and break out into the open sea. Only two ships escaped; the *Minion* with Hawkins on board and the small *Judith*, commanded by Francis Drake. Almost a third of the 300 Englishmen were killed or captured during the battle. With almost no provisions left, just under 100 sailors requested to be put ashore, where they were captured by the Spanish. The remainder sailed for England, but disease and starvation took their toll, and the *Minion* arrived in England with less than 20 crewmen left alive, including Hawkins.

Francis Drake's first raids

Although only a relatively minor incident, the engagement at San Juan de Ulúa significantly altered Anglo-Spanish relations. Francis Drake was determined to make the Spaniards pay for his defeat in Mexico, and from 1570 until 1573 he launched annual raids against the Spanish Main. Little is known of his activities in 1570, but in the following year he cruised off the coast of what is now the isthmus of Panama in the 25-ton *Swan*. Operating in conjunction with French corsairs, he captured Spanish shipping on the Chagres River and off the treasure port of Nombre de Dios, returning to Plymouth with 'forty thousand ducats, velvets and taffeta, besides other merchandise with gold and silver'. Even after the plunder was divided between his partners and backers, Drake's fame and fortune were assured. In the summer of 1572 he returned to the Caribbean with three ships, two English and one French. In late July he attacked Nombre de Dios, landing on a

Sir Francis Drake, from an early-17th-century engraving. The archetypal Elizabethan 'sea dog', Drake was an outstandingly successful privateer and naval commander whose circumnavigation of the globe was one of the greatest maritime ventures of the Elizabethan era. (Author's collection)

A Victorian depiction of the knighting of Francis Drake by Queen Elizabeth I on board the *Golden Hind* following his voyage of circumnavigation. (Collection of Clyde Hensley, Asheville, NC)

nearby beach and storming the town, where the raiders were repulsed from the city after a vicious fight with the militia garrison in the town's central square. Drake himself was wounded in the struggle. The Englishmen withdrew up the coast to lick their wounds while the French set off in search of easier prey. Drake's next allies were the *cimarrónes*, half-castes or escaped African slaves. Using their new allies as scouts, in February 1573 the English attempted to ambush a mule train carrying silver from Panama to Nombre de Dios. The ambush failed as the Englishmen were discovered by a Spanish scout, and Drake retreated back to his ships. Drake cruised off the Central American coast for another three months, attacking Spanish coastal shipping. In April he allied himself with Guilliaume de Testu, a Huguenot corsair and together they felt strong enough to launch another attack on the spring mule train. This time Drake's attack was a resounding success, so much so that there was simply too much treasure to carry. De Testu was wounded in the fight, so Drake left him with a guard and the silver while his men transported the gold back to their ships. When they returned, they discovered De Testu had been killed by a Spanish patrol, and the silver recaptured. The booty was split with De Testu's crew and Drake sailed for home, arriving back in Plymouth in August 1573, where he received a hero's welcome.

In December 1577 Drake set sail from Plymouth on his most ambitious project yet. In the four years since his return he had become

Map depicting Francis Drake's voyage of circumnavigation (1577-80). It was copied from a work known as *The Hondius Broadside,* now held in the British Museum. From Theodore de Bry, *Americae Pars VIII*, 1599. (Author's collection)

a favourite at court, and the Queen secretly backed his plan for a piratical cruise along the coast of Peru. His flagship was the 200-ton *Pelican* (later renamed the *Golden Hind*), and it was accompanied by four smaller ships. He sailed down the African coast capturing several prizes before crossing the Atlantic bound for South America. In late June he reached the Straits of Magellan, where he put down a potential mutiny and burned two of his ships before continuing. A storm sank one vessel and forced another to return to England, leaving only the *Golden Hind* to continue the expedition. By December he was off the Chilean coast, where he sacked Valparaiso, then repaired his ships. By February 1579 he was cruising off Peru, and on 1 March he encountered a treasure ship, nicknamed the *Cacafuego*. It surrendered after a single broadside, yielding a fortune in silver and gold. Drake elected to return home via the Pacific, and sailed eastwards from California in July. The *Golden Hind* visited the Spice Islands of Indonesia before crossing the Indian Ocean, rounding the Cape of Good Hope and sailing north up the African coast. The ship arrived in Plymouth on 26 September 1580 after completing a three year voyage of circumnavigation. Drake returned a national hero and a wealthy man, and Queen Elizabeth was delighted by his exploits, calling him 'my pirate'. He was knighted the following year, signalling a change in national policy. By rewarding a 'pirate' who had openly attacked the Spanish, the Queen indicated that she was openly opposed to the Spanish, making war inevitable.

The Dutch Sea Beggars

In 1566 war erupted in the Low Countries with the revolt of the Netherlands; a war of independence against Spanish rule. The Spanish quickly sent troops to the region, forming the Army of Flanders under the command of the Duke of Alba. They were the best troops in Europe, and the revolt was crushed within months, the region remaining under military rule. The Duchess of Parma scathingly referred to the rebels as 'beggars', and the phrase 'Long Live the Beggars' became a rebel slogan.

The Dutch flooded the land surrounding the besieged city of Leiden in 1574. The Sea Beggars then used shallow galleys to attack the Spanish siegeworks, driving off the Spanish troops surrounding the city. Hand-coloured engraving, c.1586. (Bibiothèque Nationale, Paris)

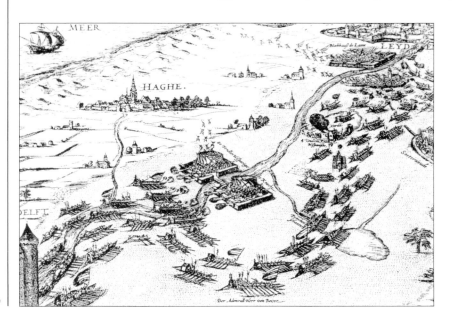

A fresh revolt flared up in 1572, supported (at least in secret) by England and Huguenot France. In April, the Sea Beggars, a group of Dutch (and some English) privateers, captured the little port of Brill, and continued to use the coastal and estuarine waters of Zeeland as a base for attacks on Spanish shipping and isolated towns. Many were former pirates or smugglers who took advantage of the conflict to increase the scope and scale of their activities. They were led by William, Baron de Lumey,

The 'hell-burners' of the Dutch Sea Beggars, fireships filled with explosives, were used to destroy the Spanish pontoon bridge over the River Schelde during the siege of Antwerp in April 1585. Hand-coloured engraving, c.1586. (Bibiothèque Nationale, Paris)

who obtained official support from William of Orange and the rebel Dutch government, although the Spanish regarded him as nothing more than a pirate. The Sea Beggars' preferred craft was a shallow-draughted Dutch coastal ship with one or two masts known as a 'flyboat' (*vlieboot*), the largest of which could displace 500 tons.

The Sea Beggars' campaign continued through the year, with several more coastal towns falling to the rebels. The Spanish forces were stretched too thinly to protect the entire coast, and as their supply convoys fell prey to the rebels, they were forced to divert ships, men and money to counter the attacks. During 1573 the Sea Beggars were reinforced by English volunteers, arms and equipment, and by the following spring they were prepared to step up their campaign of harassment. The Dutch were besieging the coastal city of Middelberg, and the Sea Beggars intercepted and destroyed every relief force and supply convoy the Spanish sent to the beleaguered city. A final relief attempt was foiled in January 1574 off Bergen-op-Zoom, and consequently the starving Spanish garrison had little option but to surrender. Similarly, the Spanish siege of the rebel city of Leiden was lifted when the Sea Beggars flooded the countryside around the walls, then sailed in supplies, attacking the Spanish siegeworks as they did so. These activities consolidated Dutch control of the territories north of the River Schelde, which for the rest of the rebellion would mark the front line between Dutchman and Spaniard. The rebellion also began to spread south of the river, amongst the largely Catholic towns and cities of what is now Belgium.

In 1578, in an attempt to stop the spread of the rebellion, King Philip II appointed a new commander of the Army of Flanders, Alexander Farnese, Duke of Parma, a highly skilled diplomat and military leader. The bankrupt Spanish treasury was unable to support offensive operations for several years, and the Duke paid for much of the army's

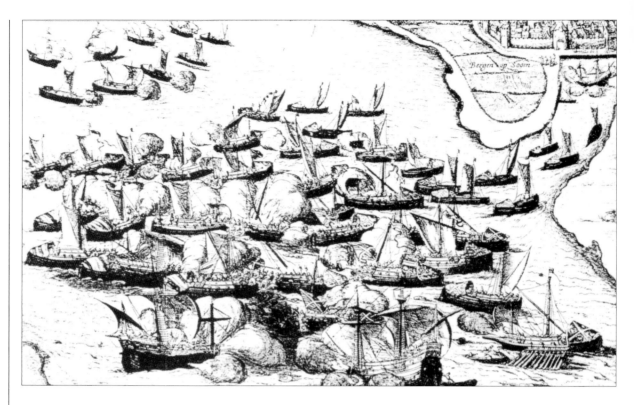

The Sea Beggars attack a Spanish coastal convoy off the Spanish-held city of Bergen-op-Zoom, 1574. Maritime attacks such as this seriously disrupted the offensive ability of the Spanish Army of Flanders. Hand-coloured engraving, c.1586. (Bibiothèque Nationale, Paris)

expenses out of his own pocket. By 1580 he had consolidated his control of the region south of the River Schelde, and in early 1581 he threatened to launch an invasion of the territory held by the Dutch rebels.

Parma regarded Antwerp as the key to the rebellion. If the city was captured, the inland rivers and waterways beyond would be cut off from the sea. This, together with strong coastal garrisons and a secure land-based supply route would prevent the Sea Beggars from influencing the campaign any further. Parma began to encircle the rebel-held city of Antwerp in early 1585 by building an 800 yard pontoon bridge over the River Schelde to the west of the city, protected by shore batteries, booms and guard boats. It allowed his men to surround the city with their siege lines, and the Duke referred to the engineering feat as his 'sepulchre, his pathway into Antwerp'. The Sea Beggars were far from beaten. In April 1585 they launched a flotilla of explosive fire-ships on the ebb tide which floated down on the bridge, blowing apart first the protective boom, then the bridge itself. Despite the loss of 800 troops, Spanish discipline re-asserted itself and prevented any follow-up attack, and Antwerp fell to the Spanish in August

The war stagnated as both sides required time to regroup and replenish their coffers. Increasingly, the Spanish realised that as long as England remained free to supply the rebels, the rebellion would continue. Three days after the fall of Antwerp Queen Elizabeth openly sided with the Dutch, sending English troops to assist the rebels. At the same time, her 'sea dogs' took the offensive at sea: Walter Raleigh attacked the Spanish fishing fleets off Newfoundland and Francis Drake sailed for the Spanish coast intent on causing whatever damage he could. A 'cold war' had suddenly become very hot.

JACQUES DE SORES PLUNDERING HAVANA, 1555

A

PEDRO DE MENENDEZ ATTACKING FORT CAROLINE, C.1565

B

JOHN HAWKINS' FIGHT AT SAN JUAN DE ULÚA, 1568

D

THE SEA BEGGARS' 'HELL-RAISERS' ATTACKING THE SCHELDE PONTOON BRIDGE, 1585

E

MARTIN FROBISHER'S FIGHT
WITH THE SPANISH ARMADA
OFF PORTLAND, 1588

FRANCIS DRAKE'S RAID ON ST AUGUSTINE, 1586

SIR RICHARD GRENVILLE
AND THE LAST FIGHT OF
THE REVENGE, 1591

H

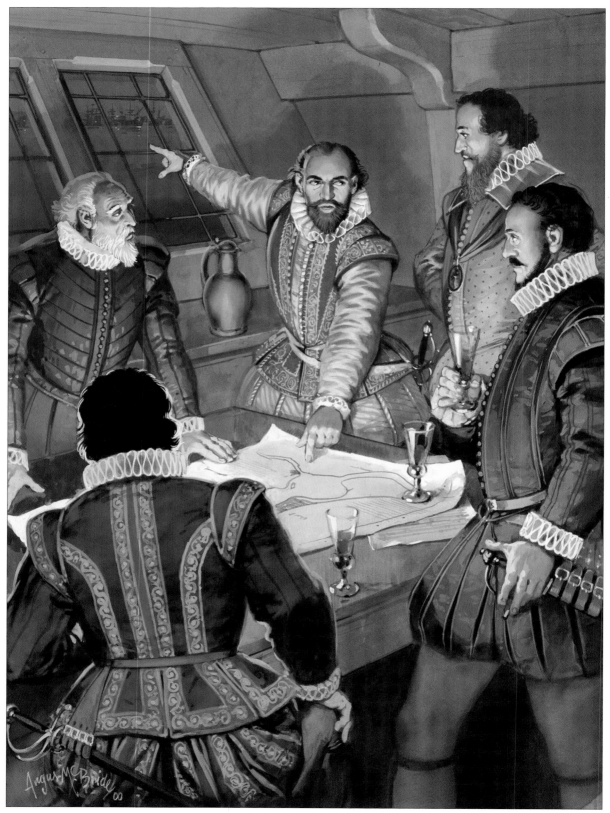

LORD THOMAS HOWARD, SIR WALTER RALEIGH AND THE CAPTURE OF CADIZ, 1596

Singeing the king of Spain's beard

On 14 September 1585, less than a month after England had sided with the Dutch, Sir Francis Drake sailed from Plymouth with 25 ships and 2,300 men effectively declaring war on Spain in the process. Drake's expedition was a private venture, sponsored by a group of investors, one of whom was the Queen. Four of the ships were royal warships, including Drake's flagship, the *Elizabeth Bonadventure*, and the *Golden Lion*, commanded by his deputy, William Borough. Drake's orders were to 'prevent or withstand such enterprises as might be attempted against Her Highness' realm or dominions'. In effect, Drake had a free hand to take the war to the enemy and secure a profit for his investors in the process.

Drake cruised off northern Spain before sailing for the Cape Verde Islands. The English assaulted and captured the port of Santiago before crossing the Atlantic, bound for the Spanish Main. In late December the fleet lay off Santo Domingo, the capital of Hispaniola, one of the richest cities in the Caribbean islands. A New Year's Eve bombardment was followed by a land assault. Drake's stratagem of landing 1,000 troops who

Drake's attack on Santiago in the Cape Verde Islands, November 1585. While English ships bombarded shore defences, a landing force of 1,000 men (in three battalions) stormed the formidable earthwork defences of the town and routed the defenders. Engraving by Theodore de Bry, 1595. (MFMHS)

Drake's attack on Santo Domingo on Hispaniola (now Haiti), 1586. The English fleet lies at anchor, and pinnaces are shown landing troops while others form up and advance on the city. Engraving by Theodore de Bry, 1595. (MFMHS)

43

Raleigh's expedition to Virginia in 1585 was a failure, and the colony founded on Roanoake Island was abandoned. The fate of the colonists is still unknown. Engraving from Thomas Harriot, *A Brief and True Report of the New-found Land of Virginia*, 1586. (MAS)

Map of the attack on Cadiz in April 1587. Drake's raid on the port was designed to disrupt the preparations of the Spanish Armada. Historians believe it succeeded in delaying the invasion for several months. Map by William Borough, c.1588. (PRO)

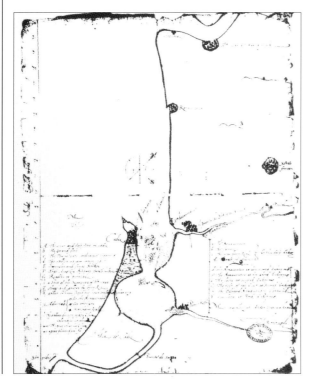

circled round and took the city from the rear worked perfectly, as the Spaniards were distracted by the bombardment. The garrison fled and the city fell to the English. 25,000 ducats were extorted in ransom after Drake burned parts of the town, but the haul was far less than had been expected. In late January the English fleet sailed away to the south, bound for Cartagena. Drake anchored his ships inside the outer harbour, then landed 600 troops led by Christopher Carleill under cover of darkness. They secured the narrow spit of land separating the outer harbour from the sea, stormed through the outer defences of the city and forced their way into the city in the teeth of tough Spanish opposition. Martin Frobisher provided supporting fire from a squadron of shallow pinnaces. After some brief hand-to-hand fighting the Spanish panicked and ran, and the city fell to the attackers. Once again, the city yielded less money and treasure than had been anticipated, although the haul amounted to over 107,000 ducats and dozens of bronze guns. Drake's plan to use the city as a base from which to attack other ports was thwarted by disease which decimated his crews. He abandoned plans to attack Panama and instead he sailed for home in mid April, 1586. His ships failed to encounter the Spanish treasure fleet off Havana, so instead he sailed north up the Atlantic coast of Florida and attacked St Augustine. His motives were more strategic than mercenary, as the settlement posed a threat to Raleigh's embryonic settlement at Roanoake in Virginia. The town was captured after brief resistance and was burned, along with the fort guarding it. Drake supplied the colony in Virginia, then sailed for home, arriving in Plymouth in July 1586. The expedition was a financial failure, but Drake had little time to brood over his losses. Secret negotiations between England and Spain had broken down, and the Spanish were preparing an Armada with which to invade England.

On 11 April 1587 Drake sailed for Spain in command of a fleet of 23 ships, including six royal warships. The Queen had second thoughts, but the wily Drake was already at sea when the cancellation of his orders arrived in Plymouth, claiming that 'the wind commands me away'. Eighteen days later Drake and most of his ships arrived off Cadiz, where preparations for the Armada were well underway. Half-armed ships filled Cadiz roads, blocking the fire of many of the shore batteries. Drake attacked immediately and captured or destroyed 24 Spanish ships lying in the outer harbour. Spanish reinforcements manned the town and the shore batteries, preventing him from continuing into the inner harbour, but the blow to the Armada was a severe one. The Queen's orders to 'singe the king of Spain's beard' had been carried out to perfection. Drake left Cadiz on 1 May, and the Spanish could only guess where he would strike next. He captured Sagres in southern Portugal and blocked communications between the two main Armada staging areas of Cadiz and Lisbon for a month before sailing home via the Azores. He failed to intercept the homeward-bound treasure fleet, but did capture a straggling treasure galleon, which he took into Plymouth in July. Then, like the other 'sea dogs', he prepared to defend England from the 'Invincible Armada'.

The Spanish Armada Campaign

In September 1587 King Philip II gave the final orders which confirmed that his 'great enterprise', the invasion of England, would go ahead as planned. The Armada had already gathered in Lisbon, and although it was due to sail in October 1587, last-minute problems kept it in port until the following summer. The greatest of these was the death of its commander, the experienced Marquis de Santa Cruz, who was replaced by the Duke of Medina Sidonia. The invasion plan was a compromise, forced on the Spanish by troop availability and financial necessity.

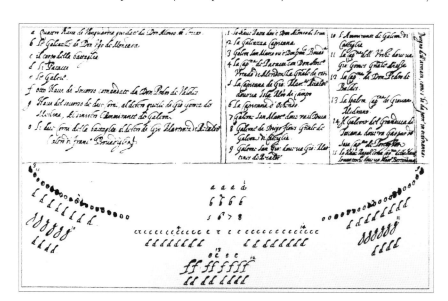

The Spanish Armada sailed in this dense, pre-arranged formation, resembling the centre, wings and reserve of a contemporary army in the field. This diagram formed part of a letter written by an Italian ambassador in Portugal before the Armada sailed in May 1588. (Archivio di Stato, Florence)

Although the most effective method of invasion was to transport the troops from Portugal with the Armada itself, most of the troops carried in the ships were there to protect the ships in combat rather than to form an amphibious landing force. The invasion troops came from the Army of Flanders, and the compromise plan required Medina Sidonia to rendezvous with the Duke of Parma and his army at Calais. The Armada would then transport the troops and their invasion barges across the English Channel to the beaches of Kent. This complicated arrangement turned out to be a strategic error, and ultimately became the reason the enterprise failed.

The Spanish Armada finally sailed from Lisbon on 30 May 1588, but bad weather forced it to put into La Coruna in north-west Spain on 19 June. The storm scattered the fleet, and some vessels were still straggling into the port a month later. The English fleet under Lord Howard of Effingham attempted to launch a pre-emptive strike on La Coruna in a repeat of Drake's Cadiz attack of the previous spring. Contrary winds forced the English to return home and await the arrival of the Armada in the English Channel. On 22 July the Armada set sail once more – 138 ships containing 24,000 soldiers and sailors. Bad weather seemed to dog the fleet, and another storm partially scattered the ships again, forcing the accompanying galley squadron to abandon the expedition and seek safety in the French ports of Bordeaux and Bayonne. A week later the Armada had regrouped, and late in the afternoon of 29 July the Lizard was sighted, marking the south-westerly corner of the English coastline. The *Golden Hind,* acting as a scout ship, sped into Plymouth with the news. Beacon fires flared along the coast as the news was carried to Portsmouth and London.

The English fleet was deployed in two groups. Charles Howard, Lord Effingham and Sir Francis Drake commanded the main fleet of 90 ships

This representation of the Spanish Armada in action off the Isle of Wight (4 August 1588) is one of a series of five prints depicting the progress of the Spanish fleet up the English Channel. Two of the four Spanish galleasses are shown in action in the foreground. Engraving by Claez Visscher, c.1610. (NMM)

Fireships such as these were used decisively during the attack on the Spanish Armada off Calais on 7 August, 1588. The holds of small fishing vessels were filled with dry wood and pitch, then set alight by crews who first aimed the vessel towards the enemy before swiftly abandoning ship. Engraving from a maritime manual of 1590. (Mariners)

stationed at Plymouth, while Lord Henry Seymour commanded a reserve of 30 ships anchored off Dover, guarding against any sneak invasion attempt by Parma's troops. During the morning of 30 July the English fleet sailed from Portsmouth as the Armada organised itself into its battle formation, a close mass of ships arrayed in a similar manner to an army of the period. Medina Sidonia commanded the centre, while the Levant squadron formed the vanguard, and the Andalusian and Guipuzcoan squadrons protected the wings. Medina Sidonia's deputy, Juan Martinez de Recalde commanded a rearguard consisting of some of the best and most powerful ships.

The next day (31 July) was a Sunday, and a strong west-north-west breeze allowed Howard and Drake to gain the weather gauge and move astern of the Armada. English ships straggling inshore of the Armada and trying to join Howard fired the first shots of the campaign, and Medina Sidonia hoisted the Spanish royal banner on his flagship, the *San Martin*. A small skirmish ensued between Drake and Juan Martinez lasting most of the morning. The Armada continued to sail on an easterly course, but its commanders realised that most of the English ships were fast, well-armed and manoeuvrable. The English in turn were impressed by the size and firepower of the Armada formation. During the afternoon a collision damaged the galleon *Nuestra Señora del Rosario*, which fell behind and she was captured by Drake during the night.

With Drake off chasing after prizes, the English fleet was far behind the Armada at dawn, and the Spaniards lay south of Start Point. Medina Sidonia took the opportunity to reorganise the Armada formation, strengthening his rearguard by moving the vanguard to the rear. An accidental explosion during the night had severely damaged the *San Salvador*, and it was abandoned off Dartmouth. Dawn on Tuesday 2 August found the Armada off Portland Bill, with the English fleet shadowing it from further out in the Channel. The Armada headed further inshore, the English fleet following and a skirmish developed which lasted all day. In several instances the Spaniards tried to board the English vessels, which maintained their distance. A separate skirmish developed in the lee of Portland Bill as Frobisher in the *Triumph* with five other ships became separated from the main fleet, although later they claimed to be screening Weymouth from attack. The Spanish galleass squadron 'assaulted them sharply', supported by larger galleons, but a combination of contrary winds and the local tidal race prevented them from boarding Frobisher's ships. The skirmishes blended into a close-range mêlée until the two sides withdrew to regroup in the late afternoon. The English were now starting to run short of powder and shot.

On Wednesday 3 August the English fleet attacked the *Gran Grifon* which was lagging behind the Armada formation, forcing Medina

Sidonia to halt and regroup around it. As the Armada continued eastward, both sides reorganised and regrouped, the English dividing their fleet into four squadrons, commanded by Howard, Drake, Hawkins and Frobisher. Thursday brought calmer weather, and as the Armada passed the Isle of Wight, Hawkins used boats to tow his ships into action, but they were driven off by small-arms fire and the Spanish galleasses, which being powered by sail or oar were ideal for use in the near windless conditions. Another attack by Frobisher was also driven off. Howard sent orders for Seymour to join him, and to bring more powder.

The lack of wind kept the opponents apart on the Friday, but the wind picked up in the evening and by dawn on 6 August the fleets were approaching Boulogne. The Armada anchored off Calais in the afternoon, while Howard and Seymour joined forces and kept the Spaniards under observation, despite heavy showers and poor visibility. Early on Saturday morning (7 August), Medina Sidonia discovered that Parma was not nearly ready to join him, so he waited in the exposed anchorage. Howard sent eight fireships towards the Spaniards at midnight, forcing the Armada ships to cut their anchors and escape in confusion. At dawn the Armada had drifted north of Dunkirk, in an area where sandbars ran parallel to the coast.

Around 7am on 8 August the English closed for battle off Gravelines and the action lasted throughout the day. The galleass *San Lorenzo* ran aground and was abandoned under heavy fire, the first of several Spanish casualties. By all accounts, the fighting took the form of a confused mêlée, fought at close range. Medina Sidonia's *San Martin* was in the thick of the action, at one point fighting off Drake's *Revenge* with small-arms fire, while firing artillery at Frobisher's *Triumph* on the other

In this depiction of the close-range mêlée fought off Gravelines (8 August 1588) a Spanish galleon (possibly the *San Felipe* or *Maria Juan*) is shown sinking in the foreground, shielded by other Spanish galleons, a galley and a galleass. Engraving by unknown artist, after Visscher, early-17th century. (NMM)

side. The Spanish were hindered by their tactical doctrine and the English avoided boarding actions, relying on point-blank artillery fire to damage their opponents. Three Portuguese galleons were forced aground where they were captured by the Dutch, and by nightfall the Armada was heading north into the North Sea, followed by the English fleet. Any hope for a rendezvous with the Duke of Parma had vanished, and the invasion attempt was thwarted.

The prevailing winds forced Medina Sidonia to continue up the North Sea coast, pursued as far as the border with Scotland by the English fleet. On 12 August he issued orders for the ships to return home by sailing around the north of Scotland, unwittingly launching his fleet into the most tragic part of the Armada story. A severe Atlantic storm drove many of the battered ships onto the western and northern coasts of Ireland, and of the 138 ships which sailed from Spain, almost half of them were lost by capture or shipwreck, taking over 11,000 men with them. Philip II's 'great enterprise' had ended in abject failure, defeated more by the elements and a handful of fireships than by English skill and seamanship. Although the war would drag on for another 16 years, and there would be two other invasion attempts (both thwarted by bad weather), England remained Protestant, and her 'sea dogs' remained at large.

The post-Armada raids

Queen Elizabeth followed up her success by sending Drake and Sir John Norris to Santander in April 1589 with 126 ships and 21,000 men. The objective of this 'Armada in reverse' was the destruction of the remaining Spanish fleet. Drake and Norris decided that both San Sebastian and Santander were too dangerous to attack, so instead they landed their troops at La Coruna and sacked the port. The English fleet then sailed to Lisbon where the Englishmen attacked ships anchored in the Tagus River and captured 60 German ships, which eventually had to be returned to avoid a diplomatic incident. The English troops landed but were unable to take Lisbon, so they re-embarked and the fleet sailed north, attacked and sacked Vigo, then sailed for the Azores. The aim was to intercept the annual treasure fleet, but the English missed it and Drake returned home, his ships rotten and half of his men dying from disease. The Queen privately castigated Drake for looting rather than attacking enemy ships, and the former hero remained in disgrace in Plymouth for the next five years.

For the rest of that year squadrons under Sir Richard Grenville and George Clifford, Earl of Cumberland, raided the Azores and intercepted Spanish ships off the Iberian coast. In March 1591, Lord Thomas Howard and Sir Richard Grenville put to sea with six warships to intercept the returning treasure fleet off the Azores, while the Earl of

Sir Richard Grenville (*c*.1542-91), who participated in Raleigh's attempts to settle America and fought in the Spanish Armada campaign of 1588. He is best remembered for his last fight aboard the *Revenge* off the Azores in 1591. Oil on canvas by an unknown artist, 1571. (National Portrait Gallery, London)

Cumberland cruised off the Spanish coast. Howard and his squadron sailed around the Azores for three months, but instead of encountering the treasure fleet they were caught by a superior enemy fleet of over 50 warships, sent to the Azores to rendezvous with the treasure galleons. The commander of the Spanish fleet, Don Alfonso de Bazan, decided to surprise the English fleet using the island of Flores for cover. Howard's scouts spotted the enemy at the last minute and all but one of his ships managed to raise their anchors and escape in the nick of time. Grenville in the *Revenge* was not so lucky, as he first had to recover members of his crew who were ashore on Flores. Grenville was unable to follow his colleagues, so he elected to sail between the two converging wings of the Spanish fleet, offering battle and giving Howard time to escape. Within an hour the 500-ton *Revenge* was surrounded by Spanish galleons and smaller warships, but fought off all attempts to board her until nightfall. The fighting raged at point-blank range, and as darkness fell Grenville was mortally wounded. He was still alive at dawn and wanted to continue the fight, but his officers forced him to surrender his battered ship. Most of his crew were dead or wounded, and the survivors were taken prisoner, although many died within a few days, including Grenville. The *Revenge* sank while being towed to Cadiz, along with several of Bazan's ships which had been badly damaged in the engagement. Back in England, Grenville was proclaimed a national hero and the last fight of the *Revenge* became a symbol of England's struggle against Spain.

Fighting in European waters during the Armada campaign provided a lull in hostilities in the Spanish Main, and Spain took the opportunity to strengthen its fortifications. Consequently, Spanish ports in the Caribbean were well prepared for a new series of attacks. In 1595 Drake and Hawkins jointly commanded a fresh expedition to the Caribbean, with 26 ships and 2,500 men. A private venture supported by investors,

Lord Thomas Howard, Earl of Suffolk (1561-1626) participated in the capture of Cadiz (1596) and the subsequent expedition to the Azores (1597), but for all his skill he is best remembered as the commander who abandoned Sir Richard Grenville to his fate in 1591. Engraving by Richard Elstracke, early-17th century. (Author's collection)

the aim was plunder rather than strategic gain. Drake attacked Las Palmas in the Canary Islands before crossing the Atlantic, but the assault failed, and captured sailors told the Spanish about Drake's plan to assault Puerto Rico. Drake and Hawkins quarrelled bitterly over the attack, and this animosity continued until Hawkins' death on 22 November 1595.

Drake launched two attacks on Puerto Rico in late November, both of which were repulsed. Abandoning the attempt, Drake sailed for South America, and cruised along the Caribbean coast heading west. He sacked Rio de la Hacha and Santa Marta before crossing to the Darien Peninsula, where he captured Nombre de Dios on 6 January 1596. Once again the Spanish had warning of his arrival, and moved the treasure in the town to safety. Two days later he sent a force of 600 men up the mule trail towards Panama hoping to find the hidden treasure, but weather and Spanish resistance forced them to return to the coast within a week. Drake then sailed up the coast of Honduras in search of Spanish shipping, but within weeks he became ill from a fever, and died at sea off Porto Bello on 7 February 1596.

Across the Atlantic a large Anglo-Dutch naval force of 30 warships and 30 transports assembled under the command of Lord Thomas Howard and Sir Walter Raleigh, with an amphibious element of 8,000 men led by Robert Devereaux, Earl of Essex. The allies arrived off Cadiz on 19 August 1596, and the next evening a council of war was held to decide the best course of action. The naval commanders decided to attack the enemy fleet in the harbour before any landing was attempted, so the next morning Raleigh spearheaded an attack on the inner harbour. In a fierce battle against Spanish ships and shore batteries, Raleigh devastated the Spanish fleet, burning, capturing or forcing aground over 40 ships of various sizes. An amphibious landing was made supported by a naval bombardment, and Cadiz fell to the allies, who held the port for another six weeks before returning home.

Philip II died two years later in 1598, having made peace with France. The war fizzled on for another six years, but following the death of Queen Elizabeth in 1603, England was ready to make peace. The era of the 'sea dogs' drew to a close, and national privateering at sea was replaced by a less glamorous but ultimately more productive era of mercantile and colonial expansion for the English and overseas exploitation and economic stagnation for the Spanish.

THE SHIPS OF THE SEA DOGS

When Drake sailed to attack the Spanish Main in 1586, his fleet consisted of 25 ships and eight towed pinnaces. Its composition reflected the depth of Elizabethan investment in plundering as a source of income. As the leading investor, the Queen supplied the *Elizabeth Bonadventure* of 600 tons, and the 150-ton *Aid*. The former became Drake's flagship, and was a unconverted royal carrack. The earls of Shrewsbury and Leicester supplied the galleon *Leicester*, the bark *Talbot* and the *Speedwell*, which was probably a sea-going pinnace. Other noblemen provided the armed merchantmen *Sea Dragon* and *White Lion*, while John Hawkins added three barks, a galliot (the *Duck*, a small galley) and a merchant vessel called the *Hope*. Drake himself included at least three privateering ships commanded by members of his extended family, while individual merchants from London and Plymouth added at least eight small armed trading vessels. Finally, the city authorities of Plymouth added the 400-ton *Primrose* and the 150-ton *Tiger*.

The fleet contained a cross-section of the vessels used by the English during the period, from large royal carracks to armed merchantmen, privateering vessels and small barks and pinnaces. The latter were towed during the transatlantic voyage, but were included to act as scouting craft once the fleet reached the calmer waters of the Caribbean. Along with the launches and ship's boats carried on the larger vessels, these pinnaces would provide the amphibious landing vessels required by the 1,000 soldiers carried in the fleet.

A reconstruction of the 100-ton *Golden Hind* was built in 1974, providing a practical tool with which to understand the performance of the vessel used by Drake in his voyage of circumnavigation (1577-80). Originally called the *Pelican*, the vessel carried a powerful armament of 18 demi-culverins on truck carriages. Approximately 70ft long, she had a beam of around 20ft, (although as her displacement and dimensions were not recorded, historians are still arguing about her size). The small main deck was pierced by a hold, and gave access to compartments under the sterncastle which formed a cabin, a whipstaff (steering) position and a chartroom all in one, and a forecastle space used to house two bowchasers and a boatswain's store. Above the cabin was a small poop deck and Drake's small cabin. The main gundeck ran the full length of the ship and housed the armament and the crew quarters, while below it, the orlop deck was used to hold stores. The vessel seems impossibly small today, but in 1577 she sailed with a complement of 80 men and boys crammed into her hull. Drake enjoyed his comforts, and his small cabin contained oak furniture and silver plate, while musicians were embarked to provide amusement. The seamen were not so fortunate, and even the officers shared a space smaller than most prison cells today. The foremast and mainmast carried two square sails each, while a spritsail was bent onto the bowsprit, and the mizzen mast carried a triangular lateen sail. The replica vessel

Representation of the *Golden Hind*, the vessel commanded by Francis Drake during his voyage of circumnavigation. Many English privateering vessels were small ships like this, often displacing little more than 100 tons. Detail from the *Hondius Broadside*, a map illustrating Drake's voyage, printed c.1595. (Author's collection)

carries over 4,000 square feet of canvas, and on occasion has exceeded eight knots. The hull length–beam ratio of roughly 2:1 is typical of armed merchantmen of the period, but the 'race-built' galleons envisaged by John Hawkins and built by ship-wrights such as Matthew Baker had a 3:1 ratio, and consequently were faster through the water.

Vessels of this type formed the backbone of the fleets which sailed under the leading 'sea dogs' of the Elizabethan period. Although Drake chose the 600-ton *Elizabeth*

Bonadventure as his flagship on his 1586 voyage, and Hawkins used the *Jesus of Lubeck* in 1564, these larger ships were equally congested. They were even slower and less seaworthy than the small armed merchantmen like the *Golden Hind*, but they provided the large gun platforms which proved useful in bombardments of Spanish cities such as Drake's attack on Santiago and Santo Domingo in 1586. We have already seen that the Spanish and the English followed divergent schools of naval doctrine. These doctrines of mêlée or gunnery also influenced the design and use of the fleet available to the two nations. This becomes readily apparent after examining the various vessel types employed by the main protagonists of the Elizabethan age.

Galleon Originally designed to transport the treasures of the New World home to Spain, the Spanish galleon was an amalgamation of a merchant vessel and a warship, with a large cargo capacity and a powerful armament. Its distinctive features were its size, with some larger galleons displacing over 1,000 tons, and a high sterncastle structure. The galleons of the squadrons of Castille and Portugal formed the fighting core of the Spanish Armada in 1588. As an example, the Portuguese *San Martin* of 1,000 tons was the flagship of the Duke of Medina Sidonia, and was purpose-built as a warship, the 'battleship' of its day. The galleons used to guard or accompany the annual Spanish treasure fleets were usually smaller, with an average displacement of around 500-800 tons. They were lower than the larger galleons, and reportedly were more weatherly. The lines of an Atlantic galleon of this type were given in the *Instrución Nautica* of Garcia de Palacio (1588), and evidence from treasure galleons excavated by both archaeologists and treasure hunters in American waters confirms the general principles of construction laid down in the treatise. While the smaller galleons carried around 20 bronze guns, the larger galleons in the Armada campaign could support twice that number.

Although not an accurate depiction, the change in warship design between the *Golden Lion* shown here and the ships of 30 years before as shown in the *Anthony Roll* is clearly illustrated. During the Spanish Armada campaign, the *Golden Lion* was commanded by Lord Thomas Howard. Engraving by Claes Visscher, early-17th century. (NMM)

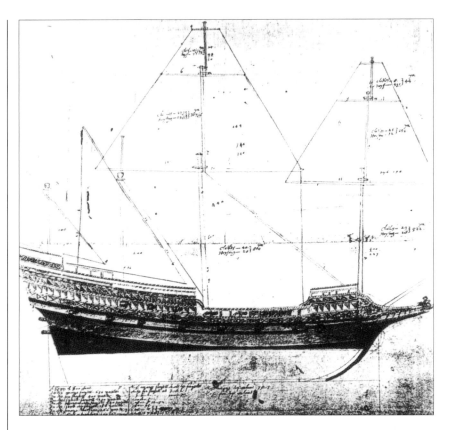

Race-built galleon From 1575 onwards, English shipwrights developed a variant of the galleon, encouraged by revolutionary administrators such as John Hawkins and master shipwrights such as Matthew Baker. The 500-ton *Revenge* completed in 1577 was the first of the type, and boasted a hull with smooth, graceful lines, designed for speed as well as the capacity to hold a powerful armament. Compared to Spanish galleons, these vessels were lower, having much less superstructure, with the towering galleon sterncastle replaced by a gently sloping quarterdeck. These English ships had a larger hull length to beam ratio, giving them the racy profile the designers wanted, powered by a sail plan which allowed for more canvas to be carried than on larger Spanish vessels. Above all, these vessels were designed from the hull up to fight in a gunnery action, not to serve as a platform from which to board the enemy. Hawkins also rebuilt the older galleons and carracks of the Elizabethan navy to resemble the smoother lines of his race-built design.

English race-built galleon hull, designed by Matthew Baker, Master Shipwright of the Royal Dockyards. The 450-ton *Revenge* commanded by Sir Francis Drake during the Armada campaign was probably very similar. The introduction of ship's plans by Baker revolutionised the production of English warships, and these graceful vessels were considerably more manoeuvrable than their Spanish opponents. From Baker's *Fragments of Ancient English Shipwrightry*, 1586. (Magdalene College, Cambridge)

Galley The principal type of warship used in the Mediterranean during the late-16th century, galleys were unsuited for operations in the Atlantic or the Caribbean. The four galleys which accompanied the Armada from Lisbon in 1588 were forced to turn back before the fleet reached the English Channel, but in several other actions (Cartagena in 1586, and Cadiz in 1596, for example), they proved moderately useful to the local Spanish commanders. They were principally oar-powered, but retained a lateen sail or two as a form of auxiliary power. Although they carried a small forward-facing battery in their bow, they were exclusively a close-quarters vessel. The English fleet in 1588 contained a handful of galiots, a smaller version of the true galley, but (at least with English vessels) fitted with additional square-sailed masts.

Galleass A hybrid combination of a galley and a square-rigged sailing vessel, the galleass carried guns in a round forecastle and on the quarterdeck, with a small broadside battery mounted over the rowing decks. These vessels were rarely used outside the Mediterranean, and the four 600-ton galleasses commanded by Hugo de Moncada during the

Armada campaign were all from the kingdom of Naples (these vessels were named the *San Lorenzo, Girona, Zúñiga* and *Napolitana*). Although their displacement made them slow and difficult to manoeuvre under oars and clumsy under sail, they proved useful during the calm winds which featured prominently during the fighting off Portland Bill.

Carrack The carrack (called 'nao' by the Spanish), a three-masted square-rigged ship was the standard merchant vessel of the era. Both the Spanish and the English cut gunports in their carracks and included them in their fleets. Compared to the more streamlined galleons, they had wider and more rounded hulls, giving them a 'chubby' appearance. Although slow they could absorb a significant amount of hull damage, as shown by the Spanish vessels during the Armada campaign, and the French fighting carracks during the Azores campaign of 1582. Carrack features included high forecastle and sterncastle structures which were well-suited for fighting boarding actions. Engravings by artist such as Pieter Bruegel the Elder have provided a range of contemporary depictions of carracks, shown both as merchant vessels and as warships, while a growing body of archaeological evidence from Spanish 'naos' provides useful clues as to hull construction and armament.

Royal Carrack The *Jesus of Lubeck*, the royal warship lent to John Hawkins in 1568 typifies this vessel type. The 700-ton German carrack was brought into English service by Henry VIII in 1545, and 20 years later was considered unseaworthy. The elderly vessel was converted by cutting down the towering forecastle and sterncastle structures, and her hull was patched before she could be used by Hawkins, although it retained the advantage of being a good artillery platform and had a spacious hold. Several of these royal carracks (sometimes referred to as galleons) including the *Triumph, Victory, White Bear* and *Elizabeth Jonas* were refitted during the Hawkins administration between 1578 and 1588. The aim was to turn them into race-built galleons, but given their broad hulls and bluff bows, this was only partially

Although the English royal fleet contained several race-built galleons, the majority of the naval force opposing the Spanish Armada consisted of armed merchant ships such as this carrack and numerous small hoys and pinnaces. Engraving after Pieter Bruegel the Elder (c.1529-1565). (NMM)

successful, the refitting concentrating on reducing superstructure and improving the sail configuration. They were rarely used before or after the Armada campaign, but comprised some of the most powerful and best armed vessels of the English fleet. Slower than pure race-built galleons, they were significantly more manoeuvrable than their Spanish counterparts, and were superior to the larger Spanish galleons in terms of sailing qualities.

The *Jesus of Lubeck* was an aged royal warship dating from Henry VIII's navy. Hawkins used the vessel as his flagship in 1568, when it was captured by the Spanish at the battle of San Juan de Ulúa. Hand-coloured illustration from the *Anthony Roll*, *c*.1546. (Magdalene College, Cambridge)

The Tudor warship *Mary Rose*, as depicted in the *Anthony Roll* of 1546. In fact, the ship sank in Portsmouth harbour the previous year. She epitomised the stolid well-armed carracks of Henry VIII's fleet. (*Mary Rose* Trust, from original in Magdalene College, Cambridge)

Hulk (or 'Urca') These vessels were used by the Spaniards as transports during the Armada campaign, carrying the military stores needed for the invasion of England or acting as supply ships for the Armada itself. They were simple, three-masted vessels with little of the ornamentation and fighting structures found on the larger Spanish ships. The wreck of *La Trinidad Valencera* (1588) wrecked off Donegal and *El Gran Grifon* (1588) located off Fair Isle have both provided information about these vessels and the stores they carried during the campaign. One vital point which emerged from the archaeological evidence is the vulnerability of the hull structure. Designed to contain the pressures created by a cargo such as grain (which expands when wet), they were ill-prepared for stresses imposed in the opposite direction, namely English roundshot striking their outer hull. The 650 ton *El Gran Grifon* was one of the larger hulks in the Armada, and the North German vessel has been described by one historian as having 'bluff bows and a broad beam'.

Pinnace, shallop or hoy The small auxiliary vessels used by the English went by a variety of names, the distinctions between them remaining obscure. A pinnace in an illustration depicting the English fleet's attack of the Spanish fortified beachhead at Smerwick in Ireland (1580) shows a three-masted vessel with a 50ft keel and a beam of around 17ft, and displacing approximately 60 tons. This is one of the larger vessels of the pinnace type, as others have been recorded as displacing 20-40 tons. The typical pinnace could be powered by oar or sail,

and most probably resembled the *patache* used by the Spanish, although it frequently served as the towed auxiliary boat for a larger warship rather than as an independent vessel. A larger version of the pinnace was the bark, which was a three-masted vessel of between 100 and 250 tons, capable of transatlantic voyages. A common type of English merchant vessel during the late-16th century, barks were frequently used by Elizabethan commanders as small warships.

Patache (or *zabra*) This was a small two or three-masted craft, with a displacement of less than 100 tons. They appear to have been lateen rigged, but were capable of using oars if needed. The Spanish used these fast vessels as scout ships, and to relay orders between other ships in the fleet. During the Armada campaign, pataches were grouped together into a communication squadron commanded by Agustin de Ojeda, who like the commanders of destroyer squadrons of the First World War, sailed in a larger command vessel.

Caravel Although rarely used as a warship, caravels formed part of the Spanish communication squadron during the Armada campaign. They were the same type of vessel which accompanied Columbus' flagship the *Santa Maria* in 1492, and were the archetypal vessels of the age of discovery. Caravels were still regularly used as coastal or short-haul sailing vessels in the Mediterranean, along the African coast or in the Spanish Main, and are mentioned in several contemporary sources such as accounts of Hawkins' slaving voyages off West Africa and Drake's raid on St Augustine in 1587. The typical caravel was a vessel of less than 200 tons and under 100ft long, with three masts fitted with a combination of lateen and square sails. As these were essentially coastal traders, their armament was usually minimal.

Cromster The Cromster was a Dutch vessel which became increasingly popular as an English trading vessel during the late-16th century. They were small, beamy and shallow-draughted vessels, initially designed for trade in Dutch waters, but capable of being converted into miniature warships. They carried fore-and-aft

Francis Drake's *Golden Hind* engaging the Spanish 'South Seas Fleet' galleon *Nuestra Señora de la Concepción* on 1 March 1579. The Spanish prize yielded a fortune in silver ingots and gold bars. Engraving by Theodore de Bry, *c.*1590. (Author's collection)

57

Queen Elizabeth's Royal Ships						
Ship	**Commander**	**Tonnage**	**Built**	**Gunners**	**Sailors**	**Soldiers**
Ark Royal	The Lord Admiral	800	1587	34	270	126
Elizabeth Bonadventure	Earl of Cumberland	600	1567	24	150	76
Rainbow	Lord Henry Seymour	500	1586	24	150	76
Golden Lion	Lord Thomas Howard	500	1567	24	150	76
White Bear	Lord Sheffield	1,000	1564	40	300	150
Vanguard	Sir William Winter	500	1586	24	150	76
Revenge	Sir Francis Drake	500	1577	24	150	76
Elizabeth Jonas	Sir Robert Southwell	900	1559	40	300	150
Victory	Sir John Hawkins	800	1560	34	270	126
Antelope	Sir Henry Palmer	400	1567	20	120	30
Triumph	Sir Martin Frobisher	1,100	1561	40	300	160
Dreadnought	Sir George Beeston	400	1573	20	130	40
Mary Rose	Edward Fenton	600	1555	24	150	76
Nonparail	Thomas Fenner	500	1567	24	150	76
Hope	Robert Crosse	600	1559	25	160	85
Bonavolia (galley)	William Borough	—	—	—	—	—
Swiftsure	Edward Fenner	400	1573	20	120	40
Swallow	Richard Hawkins	360	1544	20	110	30
Foresight	Christopher Baker	300	1570	20	110	20
Aid	William Fenner	250	1562	16	90	1
Bull	Jeremy Turner	200	1546	12	80	8
Tiger	John Bostocke	200	1546	12	80	8
Tramontana	Luke Ward	150	1586	8	55	7
Scout	Henry Ashley	100	1577	8	55	7
Achates	Gregory Riggs	100	1573	8	45	7
Charles	John Roberts	70	1586	4	36	—
Moon	Alexander Clifford	60	1586	4	34	—
Advice	John Harris	50	1586	4	31	—
Merlin	Walter Gower	50	1579	4	20	—
Spy	Ambrose Ward	50	1586	4	31	—
Sun	Richard Buckley	40	1586	4	26	—
Cygnet	John Sheriff	30	1585	—	—	—
Brigandine	Thomas Scott	90	1583	—	—	—
George (hoy)	Richard Hodges	100	—	4	16	—

rigged sails and spritsails, and their sturdy construction allowed them to carry a heavy armament. With a small draught, cromsters were ideal for operations in the estuaries of the Netherlands, and they became the mainstay of the coastal fleets of the Sea Beggars.

The English fleet during the Spanish Armada campaign, 1588

The mainstay of the fleet were the royal warships, 13 of which were galleons of 500 tons or more. The remainder were substantially smaller. By comparison, the Spanish Armada consisted of 130 ships, over half of which were 500 tons or more, and seven of these exceeded 1,000 tons. In short, for the most part the English ships were smaller and more numerous than their Spanish adversaries. They also possessed smaller crews, which placed them at a grave disadvantage if the Spanish managed to board them.

Queen Elizabeth's royal warships comprised only 18% of the total English fleet. In addition to the 34 royal ships (see table), the English fleet also consisted of 34 armed merchant ships from Plymouth, 33 from Portsmouth and 30 from London (with an average tonnage of around 150 tons), plus 43 armed coasters (with an average displacement of around 100 tons). In all, the fleet consisted of 197 ships and 15,925 men.

BIBLIOGRAPHY

Although it would be impossible to list all of the printed works consulted in the production of this book, several available titles can be recommended for further reading. These works are either still in print, or are readily available through second hand book outlets or through inter-library loan.

Kenneth R. Andrews, *Elizabethan Privateering: English Privateering during the Spanish War, 1585-1603* (Cambridge, 1964) Useful socio-economic study.

David Howarth, *The Voyage of the Armada: The Spanish Story* (New York, 1981) One of the first accounts to draw extensively on Spanish sources.

David Loades, *The Tudor Navy: An administrative, political and military history* (Cambridge, 1992) High quality scholastic study. Highly recommended.

Colin Martin & Geoffrey Parker, *The Spanish Armada* (London, 1988) An excellent combination of historical and archaeological information.

Garrett Mattingly, *The Armada* (New York, 1959) The first popular history of the campaign, and still one of the best-written accounts.

Alexander McKee, *From Merciless Invaders: The Defeat of the Spanish Armada* (London, 1963) Rather outdated although well-written account of the campaign.

M. J. Rodriguez-Saldago (ed.), *Armada, 1588-1988: Official Exhibition Catalogue* (National Maritime Museum, London 1988) Excellent overview and pictorial source.

John Sugden, *Sir Francis Drake* (New York, 1990) The best of the many biographies available.

Stephen Usherwood (ed), *The Great Enterprise: the History of the Spanish Armada* (London 1978) Useful reprint of contemporary documents.

Henry R. Wagner, *Sir Francis Drake's voyage around the world* (San Francisco, 1926. Reprinted 1969) Reprint of original source material plus commentaries.

Bryce Walker, *The Armada* (Time Life Seafarers Series, Amsterdam, 1981) Beautifully illustrated general history, but rather inaccurate and outdated.

Timothy R. Walton, *The Spanish Treasure Fleets* (Sarasota, FL, 1994) Recommended.

Neville Williams, *The Sea Dogs: Privateers, Plunderers and Piracy in the Elizabethan Age* (New York, 1975) A highly readable general history of the subject. Recommended.

Peter Wood, *The Spanish Main* (Time Life Seafarers Series, Amsterdam, 1979).

The author can also highly recommend the publications of the Naval Records Society as a source of printed sources (particularly 'State Papers relating to the defeat of the Spanish Armada' and 'Sir William Monson's Naval Tracts') although they are extremely difficult to find.

THE PLATES

A: JACQUES DE SORES PLUNDERING HAVANA, 1555

During the middle decades of the 16th century, the defences of the Spanish ports in the New World were woefully inadequate. This vulnerability was demonstrated by a string of attacks on the Spanish Main by French Huguenot privateers. Cartagena, Santiago de Cuba and Nombre de Dios were all attacked, halting the annual sailing of the Spanish treasure fleet from Spain and causing a panic at the Spanish court. The most serious of these assaults came in 1555. A French raiding party led by the Huguenot captain Jacques de Sores captured the port of Havana, the largest and most prestigious Spanish settlement in the New World.

After a two-day siege, Sores seized Havana fort and his corsairs held the city to ransom. The Governor of Havana then assaulted the city at the head of Spanish and native reinforcements, but was driven off. Sores responded by burning and looting the town, then ravaging the surrounding countryside. The French raiders singled out Catholic priests for especially brutal attention, hanging or decapitating any clergymen they captured. Finding little of value in the region, Sores and his men abandoned Havana, returning to sea in search of fresh spoils. Sores went on to command Huguenot

land and naval forces, and continued to attack Catholic shipping for another 15 years.

In this representation the French corsairs are shown armed with an assortment of weapons. Crossbows were still used extensively in the New World well into the 1570s partly because of a shortage of gunpowder. These early French raiders lacked the discipline and homogenous equipment of the later English 'sea dogs'.

B: PEDRO DE MENENDEZ ATTACKING FORT CAROLINE, C.1565

Around 1565, French Huguenots established a colony on the Atlantic coast of Florida, near the modern city of Jacksonville. An 'arrow-head' shaped fort was built to protect the settlement, named Fort Caroline, and crops were planted. The Spanish heard of the colony and Admiral Pedro de Menendez was charged with destroying this heretical intrusion into the Spanish Main. He arrived at the head of a small fleet only days after a French relief expedition reached Fort Caroline, led by Jean Ribault. With his forces outnumbered, Menendez withdrew to the south and waited, establishing a base which would later become St Augustine. When Ribault and his ships sailed south to intercept Spanish shipping, Menendez seized his opportunity. He marched north with 500 men and found Fort Caroline at his mercy, defended by a mere 150 men, plus women and a few

children. The Spanish soldiers were veterans, and more than a match for the outnumbered garrison. The fort was captured after a brutal assault, during which almost all the garrison were slaughtered. The surviving women and children were eventually repatriated to France.

This reconstruction shows the climax of the assault on the defences by Menendez and his veteran soldiers. The turf and wood palisade was surrounded by a moat on two sides and the St Johns River on the third. Bastions at the three corners provided interlocking fields of fire for small artillery pieces. The Spanish assault troops were supported by arquebus fire from beyond the ditch, and assaulted on two sides simultaneously. In this scene scaling parties approach the palisade, supported by covering fire from arquebusiers.

C: JOHN HAWKINS' FIGHT AT SAN JUAN DE ULÚA, 1568

John Hawkins was an English merchant who tried to break into the Spanish trade monopoly with their New World colonies. In September 1568 Hawkins was forced to run for shelter into the Spanish harbour of San Juan de Ulúa. The Englishmen and their five ships outnumbered the local garrison, and took over the Spanish defences facing their anchorage. Moored by their bows to the island, the English ships had little room to manoeuvre.

A few days later the annual Spanish treasure fleet arrived, and moored beside the English ships. An uneasy peace prevailed for a few days, until the Spanish launched an assault on the nearest English ship (the Minion), using an adjacent derelict hulk for cover. The English on the island were overrun by Spanish soldiers as they tried to fight their way back to their ships. English sailors counter-attacked, turning the Minion into a battlefield. Hawkins then ordered his ships to cut their moorings and drift away from the dock, running the gauntlet of Spanish fire from the shore batteries and warships. After a six hour battle, only two English ships escaped, Hawkins' Minion and the Judith, commanded by Francis Drake.

The scene shows the last moments of the English

defenders on the shore, while fighting swirls over the deck of the *Minion* out of sight, to the left of Hawkins. On his flagship the *Jesus of Lubeck* , Hawkins is depicted peering anxiously towards the island to see if their shore parties can fight their way back to their ships, judging if he can cut and run for the open sea.

D: FRANCIS DRAKE'S ATTEMPT TO AMBUSH THE PANAMA SILVER TRAIN, 1573

Following his participation in Hawkins' defeat at San Juan de Ulúa, Francis Drake declared an unofficial war against the Spanish. From 1570 to 1572 he launched raids on the Spanish Main, the first undertaken by an English 'sea dog'. In 1572 he sailed for the Darien Peninsula (now the isthmus of Panama), where he hoped to intercept the annual mule train carrying silver from Panama to Nombre de Dios. The trail used to cross the isthmus was undefended, as was Nombre de Dios, which Drake captured in a night raid. In February of the following year he returned to lay an ambush along the trail at the head of 50 men, including local cimmarone (half-caste) scouts.

Drake split his men into two groups, one to ambush the head of the mule train and the other to prevent its escape, but as the Spaniards passed the first group a drunken seaman named Robert Pike was spotted by a Spanish scout, who raised the alarm. Most of the mule train escaped, and Drake and his men were subsequently hounded through the jungle by Spanish troops and dogs. The Englishmen reached their ships more dead than alive, and Drake sailed off, only to return with French reinforcements to attack the mule train a second time, on this occasion with more success.

This reconstruction depicts the ambushers waiting on the sides of the road at the moment when Pike was spotted by the Spaniards. Most of the Englishmen and cimarónes are armed with arquebuses and muskets, as well as cutlasses and machetes. Note that most have adapted their clothing to suit the tropical climate of the Darien Peninsula and they wore white shirts over their clothing as a form of recognition sign.

LEFT **French Huguenots attacked the largely defenceless Spanish New World port of Cartagena, then burned the town. The scene depicts the capture of the Spanish governor, who was subsequently held to ransom. Engraving by Theodore de Bry, 1595. (MAS)**

RIGHT **Fort Caroline was a French Huguenot settlement in Florida founded on the site of modern-day Jacksonville. Designed as a base for raids against the Spanish Main, it was destroyed by the Spanish in 1564, and its inhabitants were massacred. Hand-coloured engraving by Theodore de Bry. (MAS)**

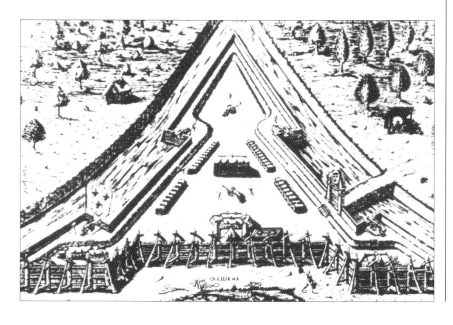

E: THE SEA BEGGARS' 'HELL-RAISERS' ATTACKING THE SCHELDE PONTOON BRIDGE, 1585

In 1566 the Dutch revolted against Spanish rule, and by 1572 the revolt had spread throughout the Netherlands. In 1578 the veteran Spanish Army of Flanders led by the Duke of Parma launched a fresh offensive which succeeded in recapturing most of the cities in the Spanish Netherlands. In 1585 Parma laid siege to the Antwerp, and linked his siegeworks by constructing a massive pontoon bridge across the River Schelde. The only hope for the defenders was to destroy the bridge and cut off the Spaniards on the northern bank from the rest of the army.

The Sea Beggars, Dutch maritime raiders who were already disrupting Spanish sea communications, undertook the job of destroying the bridge. On the night of 5 April 1585 they sailed a fleet of fireships up river towards the bridge. Each 'hell-raiser' was packed with combustible materials and explosives, timed to explode at intervals. As Spanish troops including Parma watched from the shore and their comrades tried to save the bridge, several fireships exploded, causing utter confusion. An outer defensive boom was cut, and one of the largest 'hell-raisers' drifted against the bridge and detonated. The bridge was blown to pieces, and 800 Spaniards were killed or wounded by the explosion.

This reconstruction shows the final moments of the bridge, when even the best soldiers in Europe were unable to protect themselves from this unorthodox form of attack. Their dress and equipment is similar to that used by Spanish sea soldiers during the period: practical soldier's coats and breeches with few frills. Uniformity was still unknown. While a second large fireship is shown having just detonated against the defensive boom, the larger fireship in the foreground has passed through, and although damaged and on fire, it is being carried inexorably downstream towards the Spanish on the bridge.

F: MARTIN FROBISHER'S FIGHT WITH THE SPANISH ARMADA OFF PORTLAND, 1588

The 'invincible Armada' was sighted off Plymouth on 30 July 1588, and the English fleet set sail to give battle. Over the next few days a running battle ensued as the Armada continued it stately course eastward, with the English fleet harassing, but failing to break the Spanish defensive formation. By the morning of 2 August the Armada was off Portland. While the main English fleet pursued the Spaniards, a small squadron under Martin Frobisher lay inshore, charged with preventing any landing attempt near Weymouth. When the wind dropped the Spanish commander saw a golden opportunity to destroy a portion of the English fleet and sent a force of oared galleasses supported by sailing warships to attack Frobisher.

The Spanish lacked Frobisher's local knowledge of the waters around Portland, and the tidal race which lay like a hidden river between the protagonists. Only the galleasses could cross it using their oars, and their attempt was supported by long-range fire from the other Spanish warships. By concentrating his fires on the enemy oar banks, Frobisher managed to disable the galleasses, which were swept away to the south-east by the 'Portland Race'. The Spanish abandoned their attack and rejoined the main body of the Armada.

The reconstruction is viewed from the decks of Frobisher's flagship Triumph as it fires on the galleasses. The four-wheeled truck carriage gave the English a decisive edge over the Spanish who were unable to easily reload their guns once they had been fired. By denying the Spaniards the opportunity to board their vessels, the English could disrupt the enemy with gunfire at little risk to themselves.

G: FRANCIS DRAKE'S RAID ON ST AUGUSTINE, 1586

In 1585 Drake launched a devastating series of raids against the Spanish Main. Leading a force of 25 ships, the English raider captured Santiago in the Cape Verde Islands before crossing the Atlantic and attacking Santo Domingo in late December. In February 1586 Drake raided Cartagena, where he extorted a substantial ransom and burned the town. Disease prevented any further attacks on the larger Spanish settlements, but on his voyage home he attacked the fledgling Spanish settlement at St Augustine in Florida.

A strip of sand dunes separated the river from the sea, and the sandbar prevented large ships from entering the

Another depiction of the 'hell-burners' in action, in an early-17th-century Dutch etching by an unknown artist entitled *Pontis Antuerpiani fractura*. (Scheepvaartsmuseum, Amsterdam)

protected anchorage formed by the river mouth. Drake's men came under fire from the palisade fort across the river and, unable to launch a direct attack until it was silenced, the English commander landed a battery of naval guns. Their fire silenced the Spaniards in the fort by dusk, but a surprise attack in the sand dunes by the Spanish garrison and their Indian allies kept the English occupied during the night. English musket and arquebus fire drove off the Spaniards. The next morning Drake realised that the fort and the settlement further upriver had been abandoned in the night. As the English searched for plunder they came under sniper fire from the woods beyond the town, and Drake's lieutenant, Anthony Powell, was killed. Drake ordered the settlement and fort put to the torch, then the sailors returned to the ships with whatever small haul of booty they found.

The scene is set during the Spanish night attack, and Drake is shown directing the fire which repulsed the Spanish and Indian assault. Note that the English sailors are exceptionally well equipped with firearms.

H: SIR RICHARD GRENVILLE AND THE LAST FIGHT OF THE REVENGE, 1591

Although the defeat of the Armada was a devastating blow to Spanish naval power and prestige, the Spanish empire still possessed considerable resources of ships and men. In 1591 Lord Thomas Howard led a small English fleet to the Azores where it lay in wait for the annual treasure fleet en route from Havana to Seville. The Spaniards learned of the ambush and sent a large fleet to attack Howard's force. The hunters had become the hunted, and when the Spanish appeared, Howard ordered his fleet to flee to the north. Howard's second-in-command was Sir Richard Grenville on board the *Revenge*, who waited to recover a shore party who had been filling water casks on the island of Flores.

Surprised by a second squadron of Spaniards who used Flores as cover, Grenville found himself cut off from the rest of the English fleet. Instead of escaping into the Atlantic, Grenville steered the *Revenge* towards the Spanish fleet. Soon the *Revenge* was ringed by 22 Spanish ships, but fought off all boarding attempts. The fight continued into the night, and at dawn, the mortally wounded Grenville had no

choice but to surrender his sinking ship. Two Spanish vessels also sank in the night.

The scene is set during the early evening on the deck of the *San Barnabe*, a Spanish galleon of 1,000 tons. The difference between Spanish and English tactical doctrine is shown by comparing this scene to that in the previous plate. For the Spanish, reloading their main guns was not an easy process, and they therefore placed a strong emphasis on close-range firepower and mêlée.

I: LORD THOMAS HOWARD, SIR WALTER RALEIGH AND THE CAPTURE OF CADIZ, 1596

In 1596 a massive Anglo-Dutch expedition was launched to attack Cadiz, consisting of 30 warships, a fleet of transports and 8,000 English and Dutch soldiers. A Spanish fleet lay in Cadiz roads, protected by shore fortifications. At a council of war held on the evening of 20 August on board the Ark Royal, it was decided to attack the fleet first, then assault the town. The following morning Sir Walter Raleigh led the attack which forced its way into the inner harbour, and in a hotly contested engagement he defeated or forced aground the entire Spanish fleet. The city then lay at the mercy of the allies, who stormed and captured Cadiz, holding it for several weeks.

In this reconstruction of the council of war, the fleet commander Lord Thomas Howard (left) is arguing with his second-in-command Sir Walter Raleigh (right) over the best way to attack the Spanish fleet. Robert Devereaux, the Earl of Essex (centre) commanding the land force is shown gesticulating towards Cadiz, futilely advocating that the land assault should take precedence. Personal feuds between Howard, Raleigh and Devereaux created tensions during the operation, and were typical of several of the larger Elizabethan maritime ventures, when personality clashes proved a detriment to the operation. This animosity is evident in the scene, and the lesser naval commanders, including Sir Francis Vere (back right) and Sir William Monson (foreground), are evidently supporters of either Howard or Raleigh. Note the richness of dress of the participants, who are dressed for a formal gathering rather than battle.

The attack on Cadiz, 1596. A daring Anglo-Dutch expedition commanded by Howard and Essex captured the city and destroyed the Spanish fleet at anchor in its harbour. Engraving attributed to Theodore de Bry, c.1615. (MFMHS)

INDEX

COMPANION SERIES FROM OSPREY

MEN-AT-ARMS
An unrivalled source of information on the organisation, uniforms and equipment of the world's fighting men, past and present. The series covers hundreds of subjects spanning 5,000 years of history. Each 48-page book includes concise texts packed with specific information, some 40 photos, maps and diagrams, and eight colour plates of uniformed figures.

WARRIOR
Definitive analysis of the appearance, weapons, equipment, tactics, character and conditions of service of the individual fighting man throughout history. Each 64-page book includes full-colour uniform studies in close detail, and sectional artwork of the soldier's equipment.

ORDER OF BATTLE
The most detailed information ever published on the units which fought history's great battles. Each 96-page book contains comprehensive organisation diagrams supported by ultra-detailed colour maps. Each title also includes a large fold-out base map.

CAMPAIGN
Concise, authoritative accounts of history's decisive military encounters. Each 96-page book contains over 90 illustrations including maps, orders of battle, colour plates, and three-dimensional battle maps.

NEW VANGUARD
Comprehensive histories of the design, development and operational use of the world's armoured vehicles and artillery. Each 48-page book contains eight pages of full-colour artwork including a detailed cutaway.

AIRCRAFT OF THE ACES
Focuses exclusively on the elite pilots of major air campaigns, and includes unique interviews with surviving aces sourced specifically for each volume. Each 96-page volume contains up to 40 specially commissioned artworks, unit listings, new scale plans and the best archival photography available.

COMBAT AIRCRAFT
Technical information from the world's leading aviation writers on the century's most significant military aircraft. Each 96-page volume contains up to 40 specially commissioned artworks, unit listings, new scale plans and the best archival photography available.